All Mixed and Up

Discovering the Beauty in Racial Ambiguity

Lexi Andresen Lutz

First Edition

ISBN: 978-1-960146-42-7 (hard cover)
      978-1-960146-43-4 (soft cover)

Editor: Audrey Mapes

Published by Warren Publishing
Charlotte, NC
www.warrenpublishing.net
Printed in the United States

*To Mom and Dad for giving me genetics to overthink and obsess,
and to John for being my comic relief when
said overthinking and obsessing occurs.*

Introduction

I remember running with four of my fifth-grade friends to the playground across the street from our school to play four square while our parents were inside, enjoying St. Alphonsus's Friday Night Family Bingo. It was a typical spring evening in Seattle, warm but not hot, and my friends and I were talking about all our fun plans for the upcoming summer, most of which included sports camps. We were all excited for the summer before starting middle school. As I was about to cross the street behind my friends, not hearing any cars nearby, I still looked to my left to see if any cars were coming and BOOM! A large Sports Utility Vehicle hit me. I flew up into the air, scraped down the car's windshield, and landed on the ground. Lying there on my back, my entire body was in shock.

People say their lives pass in front of their eyes when encountering experiences like this one. That did not happen to me. I don't recall what I was thinking, or *if* I was thinking, when the SUV collided into my small, lanky, eighty-pound body. I just remember lying on my back and not being able to feel anything on my entire left side.

One of the other kids, who was outside with me, frantically ran inside the school and yelled to the room full of students, faculty, and family members that we needed help. The entire crowd of people stopped in the middle of their bingo games and rushed outside, wondering what was happening that needed such urgent attention. My mom raced out of the school and fought through the crowd to hover above me, completely hysterical. That sight terrified me.

Throughout my life, my mom has typically been a stoic figure, one who does not show emotion easily. In fact, I had only seen my mom cry a handful of times ever ... up until that point. I looked to her, then to my left arm, and even though I couldn't feel anything, all I saw was blood. A pool of blood that was getting larger every second. My dad was right behind my mom, along with the large group of my schoolmates and their parents—a large halo of white faces surrounding me. I could not hear anything except my mom telling me everything was going to be okay. Everyone and everything behind my mom was completely blurred.

The next thing I remember was being in an ambulance with my mom. I don't remember being able to speak, or if I could speak, I don't remember anything we talked about. My mom later informed me that an EMT gave me a small teddy bear for comfort, and I held on to that bear until we arrived at Harborview Medical Center in downtown Seattle.

Once we got to the hospital, we immediately met with a surgeon who had a British accent, which was weirdly calming to me during this traumatic moment. My mom later told me that the first time I smiled and laughed after the accident was when I heard his voice. I somehow found comfort in his accent—so different than what I was used to hearing in everyday life.

The surgeon explained I had a compound fracture—meaning the bone in my left arm had gone through my skin. He also explained I would undergo surgery and then have to stay in the hospital for a few days. He told me it was a miracle the only injuries I sustained from the accident were a broken arm and a few scrapes on my knees and forehead. A few hours later, I woke up, happy to learn my bone was now secured in my skin, where it should be. The injury I was most upset about at that point was the large bloody scrape on the left side of my forehead. I had been involved in the school theater program and thought having this scrape on my forehead might have an impact on my ability to be cast in future performances.

Throughout the next few days, I had more visits than I could even fathom from classmates and their parents, teachers, church leaders, teammates, coaches, and other friends of my family. I had a huge pile of flowers, cards, pictures, handwritten notes, gifts, sweets, and balloons in the corner of my hospital room. While none of these visits or thoughtful gifts healed my body, they certainly healed my mind and made it much easier for me to power through that week at the hospital with optimism. The impact of having my parents in the room with me all day, every single day, in addition to all the individuals who took the time to visit, completely reshaped my memories of that hospital stay—a time when I could barely stand, needed assistance just to use the restroom, ate crappy hospital food, and felt the most physical pain I had ever experienced in my life. All at age eleven.

Strangely enough, the negative experiences I just listed do not stand out in my mind. Even though I get asked frequently where the long scar on my left arm came from, the details from the experience of being hit by that car are not what I primarily remember. The actual experiences that stand out in my mind from that weeklong hospital stay are the surgeon's distinct yet calming voice, spending quality time with my parents, the thoughtful visits from the people in all facets of my life, and the overwhelming support toward my family from the community; I did not have the awareness then to recognize it was not a particularly diverse community.

The car accident happened on May 25, 2001, and by the end of July, I was at a basketball camp, playing eight hours a day, with a full cast and sling. I put just as much effort into building my skillset, if not more, as I had prior to the incident, and I did not use my broken arm as an excuse to get out of drills, practices, or games. While I do not remember each drill or skill I learned or whether my team won or lost the games during camp, what is etched into my brain is I was not treated any differently than any other attendees at the camp, nor were expectations of me any less just because I was wearing a cast. While disability (however temporary) and race aren't equivalent, that experience—being visibly different but still equal to my peers—is one I hope can someday be shared universally by visibly minority kids and kids who, like me, look racially ambiguous.

I have historically had a complicated relationship with the spoken and unspoken differences in outward appearances between me and my peers. At times, I was thrilled to be the one racially ambiguous person in a room filled with my monoracial peers. At other times, I did not want to stand out and felt that looking different and having a mixed background somehow made me "less than" my monoracial peers—which, of course, is not objectively true. This all had to do with my own perception of myself and others in certain situations.

Your perception of yourself and how you perceive others' perception of you shape your perception of the entire world. I have always been told I have a "sunny disposition" and am a serial optimist—sometimes to a fault. Even when people ask how I got this large horizontal scar on my left arm, I tell the story with a smile, thinking back only on the good things from an objectively traumatic experience. Part of the reason I have this optimistic perspective is because I grew up in a family and community where I always felt generally accepted; however, there were certain times when I felt confused about my identity and where I fit in. This typically stemmed from the fact that I could not identify with, or be perceived as, just one race.

Preface

I was never sure which race "box" to check off on a census survey, college application, or voluntary employment application disclosure. If you have shared in this dilemma or can relate in any way, you are not alone. Multiracial identity is a complex topic that may not be discussed openly very frequently, but you are not an outlier!

If you have not experienced this confused state of mind and are simply here to learn, I salute you. The number of mixed-race people in America is on the rise, so thank you for opening your eyes and your mind to this unique perspective. Those of us who are multiracial often grapple more intensely with questions of racial or national identity than those who are not. It's easy for us to feel like impostors in our own skins, with the complexities of our heritage reduced to "either/or" rather than the truth of "both/and."

I am sharing my story, alongside relevant academic studies, hoping it will provide a relatable perspective to those in a similar position and be educational to anyone who may not necessarily be able to fully empathize.

What does *multiracial* mean?

Best Colleges defines multiracial as "having two or more races within your genealogy. People who identify with more than one race also may use terms such as 'biracial' and 'mixed race' to describe themselves."[1] According to that same *Best Colleges* article, "[t]he number of multiracial people—those identifying with more than one race—continues to grow in the United States. The most recent US Census report shows the number of people identifying themselves with two or more races increased 276 percent from 2010–2020."[2] As such, it is of the utmost importance that all people—regardless of race, political affiliation, socioeconomic status, or otherwise—understand and embrace the unique perspective of those who consider themselves "racially ambiguous."

The way people feel about themselves is greatly tied to racial identity. The confusion and identity crises faced by those who do not identify with one particular race is real and usually underrated. It is inevitable that, in today's world, individuals will encounter at least one multiracial person in their lives. Being sensitive to experiences of said multiracial individual, including not pointing out physical differences or attempting to place that person in a "box," may prevent even more identity crises from occurring for that multiracial person.

Recently, racial injustices have come to light in a way unlike ever before, particularly during the 2020 Black Lives Matter and Stop Asian Hate movements. These movements have pushed the race conversation center stage. There are stereotypes on both sides. I want to bring the conversation to light that is not typically publicly acknowledged regarding racially ambiguous or multiracial individuals. While some of us may not fit into one particular group or "box," we each have our own identity. Humans are more than just their racial identity; there is so much more to an individual's personhood.

On one hand, I grew up assimilating to White culture, but on the other hand, I felt like I was betraying the other part of my racial identity. A mixed-race individual wanting to take part in one culture versus another culture does not necessarily have to be in conflict or mutually exclusive. Subconsciously, I may have been striving to emulate Whiteness in many aspects of life—speech, dress, beliefs, and attitudes—because Whiteness was perceived as the "positive" culture. I cherished the White part of myself, meaning I was not always in sync with my identity as a multiracial individual. While identity in one's race is important, there is more to life than just race identity—passions, interests, knowledge, experiences, the joy you bring to those around you, value you bring to your community— all of which contribute to the totality of our own personhood. Let's explore the complexities of being a multiracial individual and how to reconcile the sometimes-conflicting feelings brought on by the same.

Chapter 1
Elephant in the Room

"What are you?"

It's a question I've never been able to answer in just one or two words. It's a question I've never felt completely comfortable answering, particularly when asked in a setting where I am just meeting someone for the first time. It's always surprising to me that those asking, "What are you?" or similarly themed questions, appear not to think twice about whether it's appropriate to ask that of someone they had just met.

It's a question that has always confused me. It's also a question I've never defined myself by. Although a lot of the time I might play coy and give an answer like, "I'm a human," or "I'm a female," mostly this is just shaken off as a joke, and then I proceed to disclose what mixture of races I am, usually describing my parents' different races. This response would then typically be met by some type of comment about how "exotic" I look.

I don't look like most of my friends.

In response to the question that is the elephant in the room, "What are you?", my mother is Filipino, and my father is a mixture of German, Swedish, and Scotch-Irish—or as I would commonly answer this question, "My dad is Whiter than white bread" I have skin lighter than my mother's but darker than my father's. I have slanted, brown eyes like my mother's, but my nose is larger than hers. My face is oval, like my father's, but when I smile big, my face tends to be rounder, like my mother's. Personally, I often feel as though I look like a combination of both of them, but then again, I do not necessarily look like either one of them.

Growing up, I looked different from the majority of my friends. I went to Catholic school in Seattle, Washington—specifically in the neighborhood of Ballard. I lived in that neighborhood until I was fifteen, and the population remained mostly White the entire time. All the neighbors I had were White, most of my classmates were White, and most of the school faculty was White. The city of Seattle generally had, and still has, a relatively diverse population. Other schools in Seattle also had diverse student bodies. In my small neighborhood and small school, however, the majority of the population was White.

I should stress I never felt uncomfortable in my community; it was simply the environment in which I was born and grew up. But eventually, I realized I did not blend in with the crowd. One particular memory stands out of when I realized I did not look like my friends. The moment was early on in school, around first or second grade, when I played Barbie dolls at my friends' houses. Most of my friends had Barbies that looked like them—White with blue eyes and blond hair or White with brown eyes and brown hair. But I did not see Barbies in my collection, or in my friends' collections, that had tan skin, brown hair, and brown eyes. Of course, Barbie now comes in all colors, shapes, and sizes. The time period I refer to in this memory is in the early 1990s, when Barbie was not as diverse.

Another moment when I realized I did not look like my friends was when we would play "pretend" and be princesses, and the girls in my class picked which Disney princess they wanted to be, usually choosing the one with which they could most identify. While there were certain Disney princesses with darker skin, most of them were White, and during that time, none of them I could identify with immediately, which made me realize I look different from all my friends.

While in high school, when I first became aware I was a minority as a multiracial person, receiving the "What are you?" types of comments was frustrating, to say the least. I ultimately learned to brush off the comments because I was never actually offended or bothered by them; it just always intrigued me that it was generally a first topic of conversation, similar to where did you grow up, go to school, what you do for a living, etc. I do not think anyone had any ill will in asking this question. I typically just chalked the inquiry up to people's curiosity, especially when living in Seattle, which was a generally diverse city filled with people from many backgrounds. But then we moved.

My grandmother on my dad's side was the only grandparent I ever met; she was the only living grandparent when I was born. While living in Seattle, my grandmother would visit us a few times per year from Hendersonville, North Carolina. The summer after my freshman year of high school, my parents thought it would be nice for us to visit my grandma in North Carolina for a change. Unfortunately, that visit brought a somber realization. My grandmother started showing signs of Alzheimer's disease, such as memory loss, confusion, and shortened attention span. It became apparent Grandma would not be traveling across the country by herself as she had in the past.

We were in Charlotte Douglas International Airport, getting ready to board the flight back to Seattle, when my dad asked my mom and me how we would feel about moving to Charlotte to be closer to Grandma. I was immediately excited by the idea, as I had truly enjoyed my visit to North Carolina that weekend and was looking forward to being closer to my grandma. My mom also indicated she was on board. My dad made a call to Bank of America, his employer at that time, and was rather easily granted a transfer from the Seattle office to Charlotte, which is where the bank is headquartered. Six weeks later, my parents and I were driving across the country with a giant U-Haul carrying all our belongings. I started school at Charlotte Catholic a couple of days after we made the move.

When I moved to the South, I realized the "What are you?" inquiry coming up repeatedly might have been more than simple curiosity. The majority of students at my new school were White, but there were a handful of Black students, and there was a small number of students who fell outside these two race categories. I felt that a great deal of the "What are you?" inquiries were people's need to feel more comfortable in their own skin when given the ability to place you in a "box." Once you encounter someone and instantly know what their race is, there is always some type of assumption made about that person, or at the very least, you can put that person in a certain category with certain biases, whether it be intentional or implicit. While anyone can say they do not pay attention to the color of someone's skin, that does not counter implicit or trained biases we as humans are bound to have. Individuals have certain stereotypes established in their brains, whether consciously or unconsciously, about certain races. If someone's race is not immediately obvious, then it is much harder to create a judgment on that person without putting in additional effort to actually know that person.

I don't look like my family.

One of my first memories ever is of me sitting in my first-grade classroom and being assigned to draw a portrait of my family. I remember looking at a box of crayons and trying to determine which color to fill in my skin. I remember ultimately deciding

I would color my dad and myself "beige" and my mom and brother "tan."

The day I brought that drawing home from school, I was excited to share it with my family. When I showed my parents, they asked me, "What color are you?" And I said in response, "I'm peach." My parents laughed, and I just laughed, too, because I thought they enjoyed the drawing. My parents still chuckle over my response to that question to this day. They said they could vividly envision first-grade me looking at the crayons, completely perplexed, twirling my hair, and tapping my foot as I tried to decipher which color crayon most accurately represented my skin color.

Part of the reason I saw myself as "peach" and not "tan" was because the people I was around most were White. We didn't have a lot of Filipino relatives in the area. But my mother had a cousin who lived in Bothell, which was a suburb of Seattle, about thirty minutes from where we lived. My mom's cousin had a daughter (referred to, during my whole life, as my "cousin") who would occasionally babysit me after school. My cousin was smart, talented, and pretty. She was responsible and made straight As. She was about six or seven years older than me, but we attended the same private school. She would occasionally walk me home from school on days when my parents needed her help. Even though most of the time we spent together she was doing homework, I enjoyed those times and looked up to her. On our walks home, we would mostly talk about how our days were at school and what shows we would watch after we did our respective homework assignments. One thing we never talked about, however, was race.

My cousin was full Filipino, so she had darker skin than I did, had beautiful, long black hair, and could speak Tagalog (the native language of the Philippines). I do not recall ever seeing her in traditional Filipino garb, but I did hear her speak Tagalog to her mom and dad on rare occasions.

My mom was relatively close to her mom when I was growing up. We would occasionally go to their house for family gatherings, and the main activity was eating lots and lots of Filipino food. Their home was my primary exposure to Filipino culture. Each time my family would visit, I would immediately smell the scents of delicious Filipino food: *lumpia*, *pancit*, chicken *adobo*, and *bibingka*. But apart from the food, they had decorations that were typically found in a Filipino household. I can still see it so clearly: There was an overabundance of elephant statues in all different shapes, sizes, and textures. In each room, a small cross hung on the wall; some crosses contained a figure of Jesus on them, some not. The rooms were filled with dark, wooden furniture and heirloom artifacts and bathed in bright colors and floral prints. Funnily enough, there were also giant wooden utensils on the wall—specifically a fork and a knife—which I was familiar with because my family had those in our home too. Though those utensils were not a Filipino tradition, they were the extent of the similarities between our homes.

Every single time we went to this cousin's house, my senses were awash in Filipino culture, but I still did not identify as Filipino. I felt removed from that culture, probably because once we left their home, I would go back to my overwhelmingly White surroundings. We did not have the fancy heirlooms or statues from the Philippines or Filipino food cooking at all times. Our home did not contain any distinctly Filipino decorations but instead had picturesque photos of mountains and rain hanging on the walls. I also remember having large photos of the Beatles and Marilyn Monroe hanging up in the bonus room, and my room was full of *NSYNC and Britney Spears posters, along with Lisa Frank notebooks and stickers and Barbies.

The typical meals we would eat in my home consisted mainly of Italian or American food—spaghetti and meatballs, lasagna, Italian salad, pizza, tuna noodle casserole, and, my personal favorite, McDonald's Happy Meals. Growing up, my dad was always the cook of the household. Sometimes, he would cook the Filipino dish, chicken *adobo*, and we would all be very excited about it, but this would happen only on special occasions, maybe once or twice a year. He learned how to cook the dish from one of my mom's relatives. (Even nowadays, my dad cooks Filipino food—

specifically, chicken *adobo*—more so than my mom, and he very much enjoys cooking it!)

My parents were not trying to exclude Filipino food from our home or our diets, but it was mostly just a matter of the amount of time it took to cook those meals versus non-Filipino meals. Plus, my dad was more familiar with cooking Americanized meals, and, frankly, we all adored his lasagna and constantly asked him to make it!

Growing up in a home that was not immersed in Filipino culture, and constantly hanging out at the homes of my White friends, whose homes were similarly not immersed in anything other than White American culture, it is no wonder that, while I never felt uncomfortable at my cousin's house, I never felt like I fully fit in either. I always felt most comfortable in my home with my mom, dad, and brother and with my predominately White friends.

This is not to say I did not appreciate Filipino culture as a child, but most of my memories revolve around eating good food! For example, any time my mom's cousin had a birthday celebration and during the Christmas holidays, it was a sure bet we would go to my cousin's house. There would always be a buffet-style layout of all different types of Filipino dishes. I would always reach for the *lumpia*, which is basically a fried eggroll, for my first pick of all the food. While my parents knew I loved *lumpia*, they both worked long hours, so it was simply not practical for them to make this at our home. My mom reminded me that, when I was a young child, every so often, she would cook *pancit*, *lumpia*, and stuffed *bangus* (milk fish), for no particular occasion other than she had spare time to make them. On Christmas Eve and New Year's Day, my mom would make the Filipino dishes of *embotido*, chicken macaroni salad, and *leche flan* (using her mom's recipe).

The only truly immersive Filipino experience I had was when I was four years old, and my family went on a trip to the Philippines. However, I barely remember anything about that trip besides what was shown to me in home videos and told to me after the fact, when I was much older. Most of the videos captured me singing songs like, "Twinkle Twinkle Little Star" at two o'clock in the morning, waking up everyone in the house, because I had no sense of the time change at that age. My mom informed me we took that trip to the Philippines for both business and pleasure. The business part was meeting with potential buyers of the homestead my family partially owned. The pleasure part was a vacation. My mom and dad also wanted me to be able to connect with the other part of my heritage. I had the opportunity to meet aunts and cousins; however, I was extremely young, so I barely remember meeting most of them. My mom is the main family member who keeps in touch with our relatives in the Philippines. She once told me my family in the Philippines frequently referred to me as *mestiza*, meaning "half-breed"; my mom indicated that a typical *mestiza* is pretty, tall, skinny, and fair-skinned. She said most of the family in the Philippines, along with the people we met overseas, thought I looked like my dad.

My brother, Third, is thirteen and a half years older than I am, so growing up, I tended to feel like an only child. He was usually out and about, living his own life and hanging out with his friends, as teenagers do. He had a much more racially diverse group of friends than I did, primarily because he and my parents lived in a much more diverse area of Seattle at the time than the Ballard neighborhood I grew up in. Occasionally, Third would bring his baby sister around, and I would enjoy spending time with him and his friends, but due to the age difference, it never felt like I could relate fully to them either. When I recently brought up whether my brother felt any different growing up, he shared with me that he had not always felt connected to Filipino culture because he did not learn about Filipino American history in school. He only knew two Filipino teachers and did not see Filipino Americans in the media. He pointed out that our family was not as involved in the Filipino American community. From my brother's perspective, the context of the system of White supremacy, assimilation, and internalized oppression through lack of education were also factors of his disconnect. He shared it was not until college that he felt connected to our Filipino culture because he had the opportunity to take Ethnic Studies, Filipino American History, and Asian American and Pacific Islander History classes. Much like my own perspective, he mostly recalls our parents integrating different heritages and culture through food. Additionally, he indicated that since the Filipino American experience is directly tied to Catholicism through Spanish and US colonization, the most "Filipino" culture we celebrated, from my brother's recollection, was Christmas and Easter in the Catholic Church. He also brought up that he remembered us going to our mom's relative's house to eat Filipino food.

I asked my brother what challenges he faced, if any, having a multiracial family. He responded that the system of White supremacy and patriarchy was challenging for him. Specifically, he was frustrated with the notion of constantly being asked questions as if we are an exhibit or not the norm. In college, my brother became incredibly involved in the Filipino community at the University of Washington and in Seattle, generally, even up to a national level. As such, he is ensuring his children (three beautiful girls) will be more aware of our Filipino American history, identity, contributions, and excellence than he and I were. In fact, my brother is not only doing this for his own children but also as a college professor. As a long-time history professor, my brother quite literally made history with a Filipino American history curriculum he created and has been working on for the past several years. He shared the curriculum with Seattle Public Schools, and they now offer a full-year course to high school students on Filipino American history, which satisfies the students' US history graduation requirement.[3]

When I learned about the civil rights movement of the 1960s in middle school, specifically segregation, I remember asking my mom, "If we lived back when Martin Luther King Jr. was alive, would we be on Daddy's side or the colored side?" My mom tried to just laugh it off and said we would always stay together. Her response was perfect and oddly comforting to me.

It appeared my mom, a first-generation American who wanted her children to fit in with American culture, was also uncomfortable and unsure of how to answer these questions. I do not blame her. Trying to explain a topic as complex as race identity to a child is not easy. In fact, explaining race identity to anyone who is not used to having these types of conversations can be uncomfortable for all parties involved. According to Merriam-Webster Dictionary, *elephant in the room* is defined as "an obvious major problem or issue people avoid discussing or acknowledging."[4] Multiracial individuals, racial ambiguity, society's perception, and an individual's own perception of self is the elephant in the room we will be unpacking.

I don't look like anyone in mainstream media.
Mainstream media requires people to accept reality "ideals" that are not necessarily realistic, but which people obsess over simply due to their prevalence in the media; for example, beauty, lifestyle, and fashion. Growing up, White people were the majority of the main and supporting characters in movies and television shows. Even watching the news, anchors and reporters were primarily White. Mainstream media's representation of minorities has changed since then, but it still appears as though White is the "default" character or person in mainstream media. We will explore the issue of media and representation later in this book, but right now, I just want to acknowledge the importance for children to have someone to identify with and look up to. Of course, children can have role models for reasons other than appearance, but physical traits are typically the first thing we learn about another person. You may have noticed children tend to latch on to characters who look like them as "avatars." Kids can more easily envision themselves going on similar adventures when they can pretend they are a character they physically see doing the same things. Additionally, mainstream media focuses on physical appearance as a primary attribute of an individual. Not having a large selection of individuals who look like you in the media can cause feelings of being an outsider, self-doubt, and a lack of belonging—all of which can lead to an identity crisis.

Chapter 2
Identity Crisis

Identity is defined as "the memories, experiences, relationships, and values that create one's sense of self," according to *Psychology Today*. This amalgamation creates a steady sense of who one is over time, even as new facets are developed and incorporated into one's identity ... the many relationships people cultivate, such as their identity as a child, friend, partner, and parent. It involves external characteristics over which a person has little or no control, such as height, race, or socioeconomic class. Identity also encompasses political opinions, moral attitudes, and religious beliefs, all of which guide the choices one makes on a daily basis. People who are overly concerned with the impression they make, or who feel a core aspect of themselves, such as gender or sexuality, is not being expressed and can struggle acutely with their identity. Reflecting on the discrepancy between who one is and who one wants to be can be a powerful catalyst for change.[5]

I can relate to feeling like an aspect of my own cultural identity has been repressed since I did not feel connected to my Filipino heritage growing up ... and even now. As I've progressed through life, I have reflected on the discrepancy between who I am and who I want to be in several ways: culturally, personally, and professionally. Undergoing this type of reflection on all aspects of one's life can be a catalyst for change as long as an individual has a plan for how that change is going to occur. For example, I used to avoid having conversations about race with others, as I thought that made me stand out in a bad way. For the past few years, however, I have intentionally brought up race in certain conversations to point out I am different and have a different perspective than someone who is monoracial. I do not bring up the topic of race to be confrontational or make others feel uncomfortable; in contrast, I usually bring it up to create an understanding that even those who are different can still share common ground. This has allowed me to acknowledge that being different is nothing to be ashamed of; instead, it is something to be proud of.

American psychologist Abraham Maslow is best known for his theory of psychological health, Maslow's hierarchy of needs (1943), in which he stated that individuals are inherently motivated to attain certain needs in life. In true "hierarchy" form, some needs we are motivated to attain take precedence over others. According to Maslow's hierarchy, the most basic human need, which takes the highest precedence, is physical survival. Once we are able to attain this level, we move to subsequent levels. The need for safety is next, followed by the social level of Maslow's hierarchy. Maslow recognized there is a human need for interpersonal relationships, which motivates our behavior. For example, individuals need to experience feelings in relationships that involve friendship, trust, acceptance, and love. Part of this is a feeling of belonging or being part of a group, such as family, friends, organized communities, and other group affiliations.[6]

Maslow's need for love and belonging goes directly toward the idea that people want to be accepted by others; historically, individuals who look alike are more likely to accept one another. An example of this is the "old boys club," which is the network of White men who assist each other, personally and in business, but this is only limited to other White men. Another example is that the vast majority of college sororities and fraternities in the South consist mostly of White students, unless the school is a historically Black college, or the campus has a historically Black fraternity or sorority. An issue with being racially ambiguous and having more than one race in which to identify is one's sense of acceptance becomes somewhat skewed, as there is no clear-cut race or group that may fit that individual with regard to racial identity. Of course, there are more to interpersonal connections and the sense of love and belonging besides race; however, we as humans initially tend to group ourselves superficially, whether consciously or subconsciously.

As a multiracial individual who grew up in a middle-class family in a generally safe neighborhood, I was fortunate I did not have to worry about physical survival or safety on a daily basis. The third level of Maslow's hierarchy, social, was where a great deal of my attention for survival was focused while growing up. Although I felt I belonged in my family because I have great parents who have always been fully supportive of me, there was always a small part of me that felt I could not relate "enough" to my mom's side because of cultural differences. I usually felt like an outlier on my mom's side of the family because I could not speak Tagalog, which was used on and off in conversations when we had family gatherings on my mom's side. Additionally, I would hear my mom speak on the phone to her relatives in the Philippines and Canada. While speaking the same language as someone in your family is by no means a prerequisite of feeling accepted, it certainly adds to the "superficial" part of belonging to that side of my family, which I have not been able to shake to this day.

Part of me has always felt guilty I have not learned Tagalog. For me, if I was learning a language, it was only because I was in a class for that language (i.e., I took Spanish from fifth grade through college). As an adult, I try to learn languages for places I am visiting (i.e., French for traveling to France and Italian for traveling to Italy) but have usually been unsuccessful in becoming conversational in said language because I do not dedicate enough time to studying. Also, learning Tagalog is not as easy as learning other, more "popular" languages, as there is much more limited access to free online programs and applications to learning Tagalog than, for example, Spanish or French.

I have found that people generally feel more comfortable when labeling an individual as one race or another—Black, White, Asian, etc.. We've become a race that is no longer so Black or White. In 2013, I remember reading about a feature in *National Geographic*'s 125th anniversary issue that looked at the changing face of America. The article showed a photo of what the "average American" would look like in 2050—a photo of a multiracial woman who was racially ambiguous—and discussed the beauty and acceptance of mixed-race individuals being the future face of America.[7] I remember feeling a sense of excitement and hope.

This clear acknowledgment and open acceptance of mixed-race individuals did not seem like it was the case, however, when I was growing up. In the 1990s and early 2000s, the primary pop stars for girls my age to look up to were mostly White and Anglo-Saxon, such as Britney Spears, Christina Aguilera, and the Spice Girls (four out of five), to name a few. Any kid born in the late eighties or early nineties knows the almost cult-like influence these huge pop stars had on kids during this time. Although the Spice Girls had a member of the five-girl group who was Black, and Christina Aguilera claimed some Latin American roots, the main takeaway from looking at the groups was they sought to appeal to majority White society, and White kids were those who could best relate to these pop stars. There was absolutely nothing wrong with this. In fact, growing up in a mostly White community, I felt comfortable looking up to them. The Spice Girls was my first concert in 1997, and I never felt out of place. Other pop stars who reached notoriety around this same time were Jennifer Lopez and Mariah Carey. These two pop stars almost instantly became my favorite ones to look up to, as they looked more like me—darker hair, tan complexion—and did not fit the stereotypical Anglo-Saxon look that was so popular with the likes of Britney Spears, Christina Aguilera, and Barbie. As embarrassing as it is to admit, I wrote to Mariah Carey on several occasions (on Lisa Frank butterfly paper, of course, since it was the 1990s) to let her know how much I looked up to her. I never received a true response from Mariah herself, but I did receive a generic response letter back from her fan club one time, acknowledging my love letters to her.

By 2013, I had been living in the South for about eight years, where most people perceived me as monoracial if they saw me in passing; however, most people were unsure of what race, as I still recieved frequent questions about what I was. I was happy to see the *National Geographic* article in a popular national publication, along with the accompanying photo, because it helped me realize the future of America—and thus, presumably, the future of the American South—was going to be full of people who were not only one race but were multiracial and even racially ambiguous. Until society encounters more multiracial individuals, society will generally attempt to place individuals into race "boxes."

Here's another example of society lacking understanding of multiracial individuals: during the first couple of months of moving to Charlotte with my parents, while I was running errands one day with my dad, he had to stop for gas. As my dad filled up the car, I went into the convenience store and looked for candy I wanted to buy. My dad met me inside a few minutes later after he squeegeed the windows and snapped the fuel hose back into the pump. After he asked me what I wanted, I handed my dad my candy of choice (Sour Patch Kids), and he grabbed a soda. We both went to the gas station attendant to check out. My dad paid and walked out first, and I was slowly following behind him, desperately trying to open my package of candy, when the attendant called out to me as I reached the door.

"Hey, are you okay?" he asked. "Who is the man you're with?"

I let him know that was my dad, and we were running errands together, then left. Even though I was confused by his question at the time, I did not ask the attendant why he *asked* me that question.

Looking back, the well-intentioned gas station attendant most likely thought I may have been a victim of human trafficking or just a very young woman who had a much older man buying her candy. Anyone who knows me just laughs at this story, but it is yet another example of how simply looking different from my own father has resulted in shocking assumptions from an outsider.

Another illustration: in 2020, I was at a grocery store in Knoxville, Tennessee, and the grocery attendant (a White male) started bagging my items. While doing so, in an effort to make conversation, he started speaking to me in Spanish but, somehow, also with a southern accent, stating, "¿Hola, cómo estás?" I let him know I was doing well but did not speak Spanish fluently. He laughed and stated, "Oh, I assumed you speak Spanish." I had not even made eye contact with this man prior to him speaking to me in Spanish. I was not wearing any article of clothing with any Spanish words on it. I had not given him any indication I spoke a language other than English. There was no reason for him to start speaking to me in Spanish other than his presumption that I was a member of a race who spoke Spanish. I do not think the grocery store attendant had any ill will by starting a conversation with me in Spanish, but I still left that grocery store with a bad taste in my mouth due to this experience. I was not offended by the fact that he mistook me for a Spanish-speaking individual but was frustrated with the fact that he felt entitled to speak to me in Spanish based on no indication from me other than my outer appearance.

In 2022, in a place outside of the South—Portland, Oregon—I was mistaken for being Hispanic twice in a twenty-four-hour time period. I was in Portland, attending a law conference, which was open to both lawyers and law students. I was a thirty-two-year-old lawyer at the time. During her introduction, a speaker on one of the panels made it clear she was Hispanic and proud of it. She was an incredibly intelligent woman in her fifties, wearing a bright, colorful dress. After the session was over, I stopped by the restroom to freshen up. As I was leaving, a female law student, who was Asian, approached me and started complimenting me on how great my discussion was on the panel. I froze because as she continued to talk, I was trying to gauge what discussion she was talking about. I ended up not correcting her because I felt so awkward, I had to exit the restroom and the conversation as soon as I could. I then relayed this story to a friend of mine who was right outside; he laughed and pointed out that the speaker and I were both wearing bright, colorful dresses with similar patterns. Although it was true we were wearing similarly colored dresses, I do not think something like this would have happened if the law student did not think I look Hispanic.

About ten hours after this experience, I was at an airport bar, getting ready to fly back to Charlotte. I was relaxing in the corner of the crowded bar with a glass of red wine, with my earbuds in, listening to music. Suddenly, out of nowhere, a frantic Black woman came running up to me from the terminal, along with a Hispanic woman and child on her arm. She was looking directly at me, pointing and yelling. Everyone else at the crowded bar was staring at me. I was caught off guard again in this moment, as I did not know what was happening. I took one of my earbuds out so I could hear and asked the woman what was wrong. She yelled at me, "Do you speak Spanish?" I responded, "I'm sorry, no, I don't." The woman let out a sigh of frustration and raced back to the airport terminal with the other woman and child. I felt bad I could not help in that moment, but I also felt uneasy that the woman picked me, a woman who was sitting with a glass of wine in the far corner of a crowded bar, and created utter chaos because she thought there was a chance I could speak Spanish. While I am sure the woman inquiring about my Spanish-speaking abilities was merely being a good Samaritan, this story definitely stuck in my head for the rest of the day.

As a child, when Halloween came around every year, my mom was always highly competitive when it came to the school costume contest. Many times, the options for my costumes were limited to characters like Cleopatra, Jasmine, or Pocahontas. My mom never took race into account, but I do recall a few instances when it made me feel better to dress as a darker-skinned character versus a White girl, as I felt like I could better relate to the character I was portraying for the night where you could be anything and anyone you wanted to be. Dressing up as a darker-skinned character, I felt I actually looked the part. Whenever I dressed like a White character, I felt like I did not fully look like the character I was trying to portray. For example, one year, I dressed up like Cinderella. The dress was a beautiful princess dress, but when I looked in the mirror, I just saw myself wearing a princess dress. If I had blond hair, blue eyes, and white skin, I would have truly felt like Cinderella. On the contrary, the year I dressed up as Jasmine, I truly felt like I was Princess Jasmine in that moment because when I looked in the mirror, I had much more similar traits to her, like dark hair, skin, and eyes.

Growing up in Seattle during the grunge era, I did not jump on the grunge bandwagon until around 2002 or so, but once I did, I was fully in. Like many other preteens and teenagers, I found ways to curate my identity through music. Much like most other Seattle kids during this time, I loved bands like Nirvana, Postal Service, and Modest Mouse. Again, this genre was also full of White musicians to look up to, listen to, and wrap my identity around.

I also became involved in acting classes while in elementary and middle school. My eighth-grade year, I starred as one of two lead females, Hermia, in Shakespeare's *A Midsummer Night's Dream*. Hermia is the love interest of both Demetrius and Lysander. When we watched the 1999 movie based on the play, most of the lead characters were White: Michelle Pfeiffer, Kevin Kline, and Rupert Everett. I knew I wanted to play the lead, so I auditioned for it and got it. I was so struck by the acting bug that after the play, I spent an entire summer studying the complete works of Shakespeare. All the other kids in Shakespeare camp were White, but no one ever pointed out that I looked different from anyone else. Because of this, I felt accepted in the group of all-White people. Being accepted made me feel comfortable in this environment, which further contributed to me creating an identity for myself based on where I felt most comfortable. My freshman year of high school, I attended an all-girls Catholic school, Holy Names Academy. The school and my class had much more diversity than my small elementary and middle school. I made friends with girls of all races—Black, White, Indian—and I even found a few Filipino girls whom I considered great friends. We never discussed race, and I did not ever feel that race was a contributing aspect to any of our relationships. I became friends with many of these girls because we sat next to each other in class, played basketball together, or were introduced through mutual friends, and enjoyed each other's company.

I really became hyperaware that I looked different and was racially ambiguous from majority of individuals when I moved to the South with my parents. We made the move from Seattle to Charlotte, North Carolina in 2005. Talk about a culture shock. I didn't think I would experience such a different world in my own country, but it was very different than the world I had grown up in. In Seattle, I grew up with peers who were mostly White due to the school I attended and the class I was in; however, there was more diversity in the school as a whole (aside from just my class). There was also diversity in Seattle's general population as a whole city. The diversity of the city contributed to kids growing up in Seattle understanding that diversity existed in the world, including in school, and as such, there was no need to point out when someone looked different or did not fit into a specific race "box." Unlike Seattle, in Charlotte, I was often and consistently made aware of the fact that I looked different than those around me.

As we were driving across the country, I was excited and nervous about what was next. I started my first day of school only one day after we arrived in Charlotte. I was by far one of the only non-White students, not only in my class but in my entire school and the neighborhood we moved to—the South Park neighborhood. On the first day of school, I had people asking me what I "was," making me hyperaware of the fact that I looked different than most of those in school and in my new city generally. Because of this I felt like I *really* stood out, which was uncomfortable at first.

I started wearing blue contacts at the beginning of my freshman year of high school (when I was still in Seattle) and had blond highlights since middle school. My mom had always supported my blond highlights and blue contacts, saying they "brought out my features." I agreed and liked to stand out with tan skin, lighter hair, and blue eyes. Of course, this created even more racial ambiguity as most people, especially when I moved to the South, didn't know how to react toward a girl with a tan complexion, blue eyes that were somewhat slanted, and dark hair with heavy blond highlights.

Similar to my experience, the author in an article entitled "A Point of View: Mixed Race Experience Is Hard to Categorize. Stop Trying" provided her experience related to her racial identity and others' perception of the same. Rochelle Younan-Mongomery wrote:

> In broader society, my perceived racial identity is entirely context-dependent. In majority-White spaces, I'm usually made aware of my racial ambiguity in some way or another. In my predominantly White elementary and middle schools in Minnesota, I was teased and bothered. As I got older, I had very little in common with my White extended family, nor did I speak the same language as my Egyptian family. [...] Generally speaking, fol[ks] would just really love it if they could categorize me. The human brain naturally works this way; we struggle when things can't be easily categorized.
>
> In fact, research from 2016 showed that White people with limited exposure to mixed-race people demonstrated a trust bias against them.[8] I have been on the other end of a vague lack of trust with certain people in professional settings and suffice it to say, I feel this too. [...] Alice Walker coined the term *colorism* in 1984, which is defined as: **prejudicial or preferential treatment of people based solely on their color**. As a mixed-race person, colorism shades my experience within groups and between groups in ways that are constant, unpredictable, and exhausting. I

recognize that my particular racial make-up—being mixed with White—comes with an immense amount of privilege. As a result of White supremacy, we are socialized to see the White body as superior and the Black body as inferior. Because of my close proximity to Whiteness, friends and family have said to me, "I don't see you as a person of color," communicating the inherently racist idea that the Egyptian side of my identity is "lesser than." I am foreign enough to be perceived as noticeably "different" but have White enough features that I'm still considered harmless, attractive, and civilized by Western standards.[9]

I can relate to this perspective, as I felt, when I moved to the South, that people who inquired about my race almost felt a sense of relief once I told them which races make up my heritage. This used to confuse me because it should not have made a difference as to how the inquiring individual treated or saw me. I now understand this sense of relief came from the fact that humans love to be able to easily categorize everything in life, including other people, based on exterior labels.

Perhaps as a result of this perspective, according to a 2017 article from *Newswise* by Family Institute at Northwestern University: "multiracial people have more behavioral health problems than their monoracial counterparts. They face unique stressors and often find it is difficult to connect with others—even with other multiracial people. More often than not, the parents of multiracial people will not necessarily understand their struggles. Even among multiracial people, their experiences are so unique that talking with other multiracial people can feel disjointed, and there can be a failure to connect."[10]

Growing up, I certainly felt a disconnect at times, both with monoracial and multiracial individuals. Since no one looked just like me or shared my same racial background, I struggled connecting with those around me. The act of dying my hair with blond highlights and wearing colored contacts when entering freshman year of high school was a behavior that resulted from my experience as a multiracial individual trying to fit in with the White side of my racial background. Ultimately, faking my appearance to attempt a blond, blue-eyed existence did not make me feel any more connected to my White classmates. On the contrary, my attempts to fit in actually made me feel much more disconnected because I felt like my artifice was obvious, that my manipulated appearance only highlighted my internal turmoil over fitting in with the White world. This, in turn, made me feel like a traitor to the Filipino side of my racial background. These emotions and stressors are certainly unique to multiracial individuals whom monoracial individuals do not likely understand.

An article published by the American Psychological Association (APA) entitled "So, What Are You Anyway?" discusses the importance of outside perception on an individual's racial identity. "Emphasis on racial identity does not necessarily stem from the individual but from outsiders wishing to classify the individual. These attempts at classification frequently result in stress and frustration for the person being classified."[11]

This is where being racially ambiguous gets confusing. If others do not know how to classify a racially ambiguous individual, it can be hard for that person to classify themself into a specific group.

Racial ambiguity is defined as "the term for when a person's racial background isn't easily identifiable. They don't appear to be what's commonly called 'monoracial,' or 'being of one race,'" according to the author of a June 2021 article entitled "What is Racial Ambiguity?"[12]

Racially ambiguous people occupy an in-between space in our culture. While they may be of any race or combination of races, by not being seen as of the race or races they are, they tend to have a different lived experience than the people of those races who are not viewed as racially ambiguous ... [r]acially ambiguous people may love not being clearly identifiable, or it might cause them great emotional pain. It may be their favorite physical attribute, or they may take actions to appear more monoracial. There is no universal experience of racial ambiguity. There are, however, progressively more racially ambiguous people in our country, as we become a less segregated society open to finding love and partnership in any group.[13]

I relate to enjoying being racially ambiguous now because I want to be unique. However, when I was younger, I felt societal pressure to be blond and blue-eyed due to what I perceived as society's representation of what "beauty" was during that time. Fortunately, I have since learned to truly appreciate my unique look in which others usually cannot identify me as a single race. This came from a general increase in maturity and security in my own self, along with society's increased awareness of the importance of diversity. Once I realized I felt an internal guilt about not fully embracing the Filipino half of myself, I educated myself and read many of the sources cited in this book, which helped me to understand why I was feeling this way. Educating myself also gave me peace of mind that I was not the only multiracial individual with these uncomfortable thoughts and feelings.

Another article entitled "Finally, Someone Who 'Gets' Me! Multiracial People Value Others' Accuracy about Their Race" discussed a 2013 study conducted by the APA, which found that "multiracial (but not monoracial) individuals reported heightened interest interacting with a partner who accurately guessed racial backgrounds."[14] The students in the study reported that multiracial individuals perceived people who accurately guessed their race as more likely than people who were confused about their race to fulfill needs for self-verification during an interaction.[15] In social psychology, self-verification is the concept asserting that individuals want other people to see them as they view themselves and will take active steps to ensure they are perceived in a way that others perceive them as such.

I agree with the way the students in this study generally felt; people who can guess my race are more likely to perceive me in the same way I perceive myself—not one specific race can be stereotyped or fit into a particular "box." For example, if someone can guess I am mixed and part Filipino, I automatically want to continue conversing with this person. There are several reasons why: 1) I already feel like that person understands nuances in race and has acknowledged that just because I look "different" from others, I do not necessarily have to only identify with one race; 2) Additionally, because I have always been the racially ambiguous individual in a group of my White peers, it is always a compliment when someone is observant enough to notice I seem to fit in with my White peers but also know there is something unique about the way I look; 3) Last but not least, I have a special place in my heart for my Filipino heritage, even though I have not always felt fully connected to this part of my heritage for most of my life. When someone—particularly someone in the South—can identify I am part Filipino, I am always pleasantly surprised, as the population of Filipinos in the South, and specifically in Charlotte, is incredibly small. This occurrence is rare in Charlotte, but I have had great conversations with people who have correctly guessed I am part Filipino. Because there is such a minuscule population of Filipino Americans in the South generally, I feel even more bonded to anyone I meet in the South who is Filipino.

The 2013 APA study was the first published study conducted to determine how multiracial individuals perceive others' perception of themselves and how that would likely affect subsequent interactions with those same individuals. The article further pointed out that "psychologists have paid little attention to how multiracial individuals feel about different racial labels applied to them" and added that "multiracial people encounter different views about their race in different situations,"[16] which, in my experience, is true.

While living in Seattle, I received very few inquiries about my race; however, when I moved to the South, it was continuously a topic of conversation, particularly for those whom I had just met for the first time, presumably because the South is much less diverse and not used to seeing people whose race they cannot immediately identify. The same article states, "[m]ultiracial individuals of both

White and minority ancestry, for example, may be mistakenly perceived as monoracial members of their minority groups ... In other situations, multiracial people encounter confusion about their race from others because they are more likely than monoracial people to be racially ambiguous."[17]

This happened to me repeatedly when I first moved to the South and still occurs today.

The study from the same article found that "[m]ultiracial people are stereotyped as less socially skilled than monoracial people because they are rejected by both majority and minority groups in society," and "[m]ultiracial people feel pressured by others to identify with traditional racial categories that fail to capture their racial complexity, particularly in situations in which others express confusion about their race."[18]

I feel pressure to identify with traditional racial categories, especially in the South, primarily because of the number of questions I receive about my race.

The article further pointed out that: "[m]ultiracial people dislike interaction with people who incorrectly categorize them as members of the wrong ethnic or cultural groups because of social identity threat, which is the experience of being categorized in a manner inconsistent with one's self-perceptions."[19]

The potential lack of social interaction could have something to do with the fact that multiracial people have struggled with being pressured to identify with a traditional race category to fit into a particular "box," but they do not know where to fit, which could then come off as lack of social skills. Sadly, the article notes that "[m]ultiracial people regard race as an aspect of the self—requiring verification from others."[20] This is likely why the study found that multiracial people value accurate judgments of those who can correctly identify their race(s) because those people verify that their own self-perceptions are true.

Overall, this study demonstrates that multiracial individuals experience a plethora of emotions when it comes to others identifying their race(s); therefore, it is important for everyone to understand the nuances of others' racial backgrounds, particularly since we live in a world in which multiracial people someday will be the norm as we continue forward.

A January 2020 study published in *Society for Personality and Social Psychology* entitled "The Racial Identities Multiracial People Adopt May Depend on How Others Treat Them" specifically found that "other peoples' comments and questions about appearance, as well as perceived discrimination from certain racial groups, relate to how strongly mixed-race people identify as multiracial."[21] Those conducting the study wanted to answer questions about why some people who are of more than one race claim a "multiracial" identity more strongly than other mixed-race individuals do. The study found that mixed-race individuals more strongly identified with being multiracial if third parties expressed surprise at that individual's particular race make-up.[22]

This is true for me too. When people are surprised by my racial makeup—which is typically the case—I feel I more strongly identify with being multiracial. In the study conducted in January 2020, those conducting the study were interested to learn why some mixed-race individuals claim a multiracial identity more strongly than other mixed-race people. The study found the following:

> Participants who received feedback that their racial appearance was inconsistent with their background more strongly identified as multiracial than those who did not experience such feedback. So, if many people tell Olivia they are surprised she has both Black and White racial ancestry, this increases the chances of Olivia strongly identifying as multiracial. Racial identity is more than a collection of boxes people check on a survey—it can serve as a form of social connection with others and offer people a deep sense of meaning. Consistent with the idea that race is a social construct, our findings highlight the interpersonal and social elements related to how strongly mixed-race individuals' identify as multiracial. So, before asking questions such as "What are you" or "Wait, are you Latina," consider how the comments we direct

toward others could have unintended psychological implications. Curiosity is normal, but if you really wish to get to know a person, it might be a good idea to wait for them to bring up the important question of race and identity. In today's increasingly multiracial world, it might be equally important to not assume a person's physical appearance is always strongly linked to their racial identity.[23]

As a mixed-race person, this phenomenon where mixed-race individuals can so easily change their own self-identification simply because of reactions from or perceptions by others does not surprise me. The world in which I grew up did not initially accept multiracial individuals and racially ambiguous as readily as monoracial individuals, without expressing confusion or pointing out how such individuals look different than others.

Chapter 3
Pass or Fail

Why is it important for multiracial individuals to identify with our respective race(s)? A study called "Summary of Stages of Racial Identity Development," published by the Interaction Institute for Social Change (IISC), discusses the stages of establishing identity for biracial individuals. Specifically, the study reveals the theory of racial identity development as proposed by W. S. Carlos Poston.

1. PERSONAL IDENTITY: sense of self unrelated to ethnic grouping; occurs during childhood
2. CHOICE OF GROUP: as a result of multiple factors, individuals feel pressured to choose one racial or ethnic group identity over another
3. CATEGORIZATION: choices influenced by status of the group, parental influence, cultural knowledge, appearance
4. ENMESHMENT/DENIAL: guilt and confusion about choosing an identity that isn't fully expressive of all their cultural influences; denial of differences between the racial

groupings; possible exploration of the identities not chosen in stages 2 and 3

5. APPRECIATION: of multiple identities
6. INTEGRATION: sense of wholeness, integrating multiple identities[24]

Based on this theory, an individual's own self-identification has more to do with how that individual's peers and community view them. This demonstrates how powerful the mind is and how much of an influence society's perception—or even what society's *perceived* perception is—on a person, specifically someone who already has issues identifying with just one race based on looking at society versus in the mirror.

A 2015 publication, revealing survey results from Pew Research Center, found:

> For multiracial adults, the intersection of race and social connections is complicated. Many mixed-race adults straddle two (or more) worlds, and their relationships reflect that. Whether it is in the friendships they form, the neighborhood where they live, or contact with family members, interactions with the racial groups that make up their background are often uneven, as is the level of acceptance multiracial adults feel they get from each group … [a] majority of Americans say they have at least some close friends who are White, Black, Hispanic, or mixed race. And somewhat smaller shares say they have close friends who are Asian and American Indian. Multiracial adults are more likely than the general public to say at least some of their close friends are mixed race, Black, or American Indian. In fact, one-in-six (16 percent) multiracial adults say all or most of their close friends are multiracial, compared with only 6 percent of the general public.[25]

The article further points out:

> While friendship clearly transcends race and ethnicity, the two
> are strongly correlated. Individuals tend to have more friends
> among their own race group than they do among races different
> than their own. [...] There's no question the US is becoming
> more racially and ethnically diverse. Still, the survey finds that
> relatively few adults say they have a lot in common with those
> who don't share their own racial background. This is especially
> true of adults who are only one race. Among those who are single-
> race White, 62 percent say they have a lot in common with people
> in the US who are White, while about one-in-ten or fewer say
> they have a lot in common with people who are Black, Asian, or
> American Indian. The pattern is similar for adults who are single-
> race Black or Asian.[26]

This could be part of the reason why multiracial individuals face
confusion and social anxiety more so than monoracial individuals—
they are not sure where they fit into friendship relationships, as well
as within their own families.

Starting school in the South, I received more "What are you?"
and "you're so exotic" inquiries than ever before in my life.
Around the third month after moving down, I started asking those
questioning to guess, as if it was some sort of game. Answers I
received from others ranged anywhere from Greek to Spanish to
Hawaiian to Haitian. It was rare anyone would ever guess my
actual race, which was absolutely fine. I didn't expect anyone to.
The amount of half-Filipino, half-White people in Charlotte, North
Carolina was extremely minimal at that time, and it still is.

Almost all the close friends I made in high school were White.
They never made me feel any different. When I stopped wearing
my blue contacts in 2006, they became a distant memory and a
joke my friends and I would talk about. But no one ever made any
reference to race or how the contacts potentially made me more
racially ambiguous. I always felt completely comfortable and at

home with them and their families. I wasn't questioned about my race as much when with a group of White girls. I received questions about what race I am more frequently when I was singled out as the "new girl" but did not receive the same inquiry as much when I was part of a group of all-White girls. As my brother would routinely tell me, I could "pass" for White.

When I started applying to colleges, I knew I wanted to stay in the South because I fell in love with the weather and people. I had made some great friends in Charlotte, and my parents were still living in the area at the time. I applied to a variety of colleges in the South, most of which were a few hours from Charlotte. By the time I was a senior in high school, my brother was a professor at the University of Washington. He had to twist my arm to even put in my application at UW because the thought of returning to Seattle was not personally appealing to me. The fact that I had grown up as a young child surrounded by mostly White peers, combined with moving to Charlotte—which was much less diverse than Seattle—had created a sort of "safety zone" in which I felt I was more accepted in majority White environments. I also applied to Penn State University, my father's alma mater, which was the first university to which I was accepted. Again, this wasn't the South, and I felt at home in the South, so I decided not to attend either UW or Penn State. Ultimately, I ended up at the University of North Carolina Wilmington, which was a highly desirable college because of its location about five minutes away from Wrightsville Beach. It was also only about three and a half hours from Charlotte, which was close enough to my parents to be able to drive home but far enough away that I didn't feel like I should come visit them every weekend. The best of both worlds for most new college students.

"UNC-White" was the nickname some college students gave to my college, which was located on the coast of North Carolina and, as you can guess, did not have a particularly diverse population. Greek life was not as big at UNCW as it was at some other schools, but my mom had always encouraged me to join a sorority because of the lifelong friends and networking opportunities she knew they would bring. I also saw it as an instant in to my "safe zone," having a group of girls I could befriend and bond with who were similar in appearance and experience to the groups of friends I had grown up with. Going through rush in fall 2012, the vast majority of girls going through recruitment were White. I do remember the "What are you?" question coming up a couple of times during recruitment but not quite as much as when I started high school in the South. I do recall one girl in a certain sorority immediately asking me, very first thing, whether I was "Lumbee Indian" (a Native American tribe of North Carolina). Then she immediately followed up with the fact that her boyfriend was Lumbee Indian. I wasn't 100 percent sure how to feel and, as usual, just laughed off her comment.

I ended up joining Phi Mu Fraternity, which prided itself on being the second-oldest sorority in the country, with its headquarters in Peachtree, Georgia. I loved every moment of being a member of Phi Mu. In our "Phi" (new member) class photo, I am one of two non-White girls, but this did not bother me. My race would rarely come up. Again, I was rarely questioned when out with my sorority sisters. I could "pass" for White, particularly when I was surrounded by a group of them.

I was, however, made hyperaware of the fact that I looked different at certain times in college. For example, there was an online board called "College Anonymous Confession Board" or "College ACB" for short. This website started in 2008—the same year I started college—and allowed students from colleges all around the country to anonymously post anything on the website—most of which consisted of rumors, gossip, rants, and hateful discussions about people and organizations at colleges.[27] This website was particularly popular among Greek life at UNCW, which was a very small percentage of the student body at that time. My sorority sisters and I would occasionally take a look on the website just to see what people were saying about our sorority and other sororities and fraternities on campus. It was one of those websites you knew was a waste of time to even look at, but sometimes you couldn't help yourself. When reading through comments, we never took anything too seriously, and we laughed at the negative posts about our sorority as we read them together. In our minds, the justification to view the negative comments as humorous was that whoever was posting was probably a girl in another sorority who was jealous and just trying to bring us down.

Looking back, this website was toxic and led to much more hate and many more negative experiences for individuals than anything else. Nothing on the website was meant to be positive or helpful; it mostly entailed gossip, sexual jokes and objectification of women, and general hatred. One night, during the first semester freshman year, I was getting ready in my dorm room to meet my friends at a party, and I became curious as to whether anyone had mentioned my name on College ACB. When I searched my name, a result came up, and it was actually an entire thread entitled "Lexi Andresen," and the body of the thread only said two words: "Asian Persuasion." One of the anonymous comments that stuck out to me was vulgar and only asked, "Is it true that Asians have slanted vaginas?" There were about eight other anonymous comments on the thread named after me which I thankfully do not recall in detail, but I do remember all the comments were either objectifying or criticizing my body or my appearance generally. This was one of the first experiences in my life where I felt directly attacked because of my Filipino heritage. The fact that someone had created a thread on this website about me and only narrowed the discussion down to my race was difficult for me to understand at that time. After reading this thread, I was upset and felt I needed to talk to someone about what was written.

That night, I told a couple of my closest sorority sisters about what I discovered on College ACB. When I was venting to my friends about what I saw, I did not focus so much on the fact that someone called me "Asian" or made a vulgar comment but mostly let them know I was distressed about the fact that someone would go out of their way to create an entire thread with my name on it. At this point in time, I had only been in college for about three months. My friends empathized with me and reminded me this is why we do not search our own names or our sorority on that toxic site. They also gave me a helpful reminder that everyone who posts on that website are cowards. All three of us made a pact to never go on the site again. To this day, I have no idea who started the thread or wrote anything about me on that awful website. I realized that whoever wrote about me, and the following comments, were likely people I've never even met or had any type of substantive conversation with, as I truly believe those people with whom I shared real relationships in college would never define me simply based on one-half of my heritage nor open it up for discussion on that treacherous website. I did not go on the website ever again. College ACB garnered a great deal of attention during the rest of my college years due to the controversy it caused in colleges and specifically the concern over mental health issues it likely caused with college students. The website no longer exists.

Around this same time—first semester of freshman year—I had a core girlfriend group outside my sorority, all of whom were also freshman, and we went out socially a few times per month. These were the group of girls I made friends with prior to rushing my sorority, and I love how we still made it a point to go out together, even when we joined different sororities and other organizations. This group consisted of about eight girls—six of whom were fully White, myself, and one girl who was Korean; we will call her Diana. Diana would frequently come up to me when we saw each other, laughing, saying someone mistook her for me while she was on campus, walking to class. I found this interesting because, during the entirety of my time in college, no one had ever mistaken me for Diana. For some reason, it was only people mistaking her for me. I am not sure of the reason for this, but I always thought it was strange.

During our first year of college, Diana was mistaken for me at least once, if not twice, per day. Every time I saw Diana, she would tell me a new person called her by my name. As the years went by in college, and we both got to know more people, this confusion decreased, but even through senior year of college, people were still mistaking Diana for me. This is not the fault of anyone who called Diana by name. The majority of the White population and general White culture at my college was the reason for the fact that one of the handful of Asian girls on campus was repeatedly mistaken to be another half-Asian girl on campus. Diana and I generally just joked about the fact that we were the "token Asians" in the group of White girls and at our college generally; however, we never talked about any racism we had experienced or feelings surrounding our identity. This topic was not something we felt comfortable talking about with each other during this time, particularly since most of the time, when we were together, it was with our other White girlfriends.

When I was deciding what to major in college, I chose political science. It's a very stereotypical story, as I made this decision when I was sitting in my required political science class freshman year. I had always been fascinated with politics and the law. While I had never considered law school before taking this class, I realized that studying something I was interested in would be a great first step. After many conversations with my parents, friends, professors, and career counselors at school, I became more and more intrigued with the idea of being a problem-solver and an advocate and decided my best bet was to major in political science, take the LSAT, and go to law school after I graduated. I didn't know what type of lawyer I wanted to be, but I decided I was definitely going to be one.

Not only did the law fascinate me, but I also appreciated the different perspective I would be bringing to the table as a mixed-race female attorney, something that was not stereotypical during this time, as most lawyers who had notariety during that time were older, White males. In 2012, the year I started law school, women and minorities were going to law school and becoming lawyers at a rate higher than in the past, but the field was still something that was considered a White, male–dominated profession. As many other girls who attended law school during my time, one of my role models was Elle Woods from the movie *Legally Blonde*. Elle Woods was another walking contradiction—a sorority girl turned

Harvard Law School graduate. I looked up to her. Again, another blond-haired, blue-eyed character in pop culture I was identifying with. As I went to college and joined a sorority whose colors were pink and white (Elle Woods was obsessed with pink), I created an identity for myself based on Elle's character.

During college, I also became involved in many "majority White" clubs and organizations (in addition to already being in a traditional sorority). These included College Republicans and Pre-Law Society. These organizations had very little diversity, if any. Whether it was intentional, I was creating an atmosphere for myself to further be surrounded by mostly White people; this created a sense of comfort for me because of how I grew up—being surrounded by majority White peers—and what was portrayed as acceptable in society and the media.

Looking back, I did not even bother searching for any Filipino or Asian American clubs in college because I assumed none existed. Today, UNCW has an "Asian Student Association," which I would not have identified with during that time of my life because I did not consider myself fully Asian. Of course, I am sure there are students who are members of this organization who are only part Asian, but it did not occur to me to even consider that. All I know is I would not have felt comfortable in a setting where everyone was Asian. I attribute this to the environment in which I grew up, along with my eventual move to the South, which only increased the number of White peers I was surrounded by, along with the hyperawareness I developed upon moving to the South.

According to the article in *Newswise*, "[f]or multiracial people, imposter syndrome goes deeper than our ability to compete with others in skills or knowledge. It can affect our cultural and ethnic identity. When you don't feel like you 'belong' to a group of people, it can make you question your experiences and sense of identity, especially when how [you] identify is often rooted in the way the world sees you."[28]

While I was at "UNC-White," even though the majority of the population was White, I did feel a sense of belonging. I had been happy there and was thrilled with the friendships I made and organizations I joined. But in the back of my mind, there was always a feeling I was missing something, that I was not properly connecting with a part of myself—a part I felt like I was betraying. When I was with individuals who were Asian or Filipino, I no longer felt as though I could fit in, or I was somehow an "impostor" in my own skin and to my own culture. Much of this came from the fact that I did not look particularly Asian nor inherently White. I was, and am, somewhere in between.

Race is uniquely complex because individuals like to use race as something to identify themselves and connect to their ancestry; however, when an individual is judged based solely on race, animosity and misunderstanding is typically the result. Race should be looked at as an immutable characteristic on which one should not be judged—similar to shoe size: everyone has one, but no one should necessarily be judged or assigned certain traits or characteristics based only on shoe size. At the same time, because individuals enjoy identifying with a race and connecting it back to family, history, and ancestry, it is, of course, more important than something as straightforward as a shoe size. How do we reconcile these two juxtapositions? I think the happy medium is an individual's race is what it is (again, similar to shoe size), and the amount of connection an individual has to that person's race—or multiple races—should be up to that individual to decide. No one else should be assigning judgment as to how much someone should be interested in, or in tune with, one's race. Although race is part of one's being, it does not and should not define an individual. It does not have to be a huge part of one's identity—or it can be, if it's something that person values. For example, if someone was raised to believe culture was to be a large part of someone's values, then naturally, race may be a large part of one's identity. This is separate and apart from race as only a physical characteristic. There is a difference between race as a physical characteristic and culture in defining one's values and identity. Although race and culture can certainly play a part in one's personality, life experiences, knowledge, and emotions, it need not form the basis for one's entire identity.

A study from the Pew Research Institute in June 2015 found that:

> [W]hen asked why they don't identify as multiracial, about half (47 percent) say it is because they look like one race. An identical proportion say they were raised as one race, while about four-in-ten (39 percent) say they closely identify with a single race. And about a third (34 percent) say they never knew the family member or ancestor who was a different race. (Individuals were allowed to select multiple reasons.) This multiracial "identity gap" plays out in distinctly different ways in different mixed-race groups. [...] [M]any mixed-race Americans say that over the course of their lifetimes, they have changed how they viewed their racial identity. According to the survey, about three-in-ten mixed-race adults (29 percent) who now report more than one race for themselves say they used to see themselves as just one race. But among those who did not report more than one race for themselves in this survey—instead are included in the multiracial group because of the races they reported for their parents or grandparents—an identical share have switched their racial identity: 29 percent say they once saw themselves as more than one race but now see themselves as one race.[29]

Being multiracial is complicated in the sense that a multiracial individual, in particular those who are racially ambiguous, tend to identify with different races throughout that individual's lifetime. Personally, I initially strongly identified with my White heritage due to the environment in which I grew up and the way others interacted with me, not necessarily acting like I was different than those around me. When I moved to the South, I became hyperaware of my Filipino heritage because of the fact that people more frequently pointed out I looked different. At present, I am learning to appreciate and embrace both sides of my heritage and identify with both equally.

Interestingly, "[a]mong those who report that they themselves are two or more races, about six-in-ten (63 percent) identify as multiracial. But even for this group, roughly a third (36 percent) do not consider themselves mixed race." Further, "[a]ccording to the survey, only 9 percent of all multiracial adults believe they are perceived as a mix of races by others."[30]

I agree that only a small percentage of multiracial people believe they are perceived as a mix of races by others since people in society automatically assume individuals who do not "look White" must be of a completely different race. I think the perception of everyone being monoracial is slowly fading; however, society's default tends to be that everyone is, and only identifies with, one race. In general, mixed-race individuals are still an anomaly.

The same study noted, "[a]t some point in their lives, about one-in-five multiracial adults (21 percent) have dressed or behaved in a certain way in order to influence how others saw their race."[31]

This was reminiscent of my blue contacts along with blond highlights, which I started to do when I lived in Seattle. At that point in my life, I believed others perceived me as White, and therefore, I had blond highlights and blue contacts to further influence how others saw my race.

Interestingly, the study goes on to find that "[a]bout one-in-five multiracial adults (21 percent) say they have felt pressure from friends, family, or society in general to choose one of the races in their background over another."[32]

This is not surprising to me, as most people feel most comfortable when they are able to put others in a "box" and, therefore, make perceptions about those individuals without actually getting to know them. Placing people in "boxes" for purposes of efficient judgment of others is not how humans should treat other humans. From my own personal experience, I have not felt pressure from family or friends to choose one race in my background over another; however, I have certainly felt pressure from society when I hear others ask me what I am and see checkboxes for race on applications in which only one race can be selected—as if I should only be defined by one race. This was the world in which I grew up. In more recent years, I have noticed there are more options for selecting race, including the ability to check multiple squares: "Two or More Races," "Other," and "Multiracial." Although these options do not perfectly describe the heritage of individuals who are more than one race, it is a start in acknowledging that not all of us can fit into just one checkbox.

Another Pew Research study goes on to take note of the issue of discrimination:

> [Y]et, while the survey finds a generally positive outlook among multiracial adults, considerable shares report that they have experienced discrimination because of their racial background, including fully 55 percent who say they have been subject to slurs or jokes, about four-in-ten (43 percent) who say they have received poor service in restaurants and other businesses, and a third or less who have been treated unfairly by an employer in hiring, pay, or promotion (33 percent); have been threatened or physically attacked (30 percent); or have been unfairly stopped by police (25 percent). Experiences with discrimination are, at least in part, tied to the way one's racial background is perceived by others. Multiracial adults who are seen by others as White are far less likely to say they have faced discrimination across several measures than those who are seen as Black, Hispanic, or multiracial.[33]

In most instances, I am a White-passing multiracial individual. Therefore, I am less likely to attribute poor treatment by others based on my race versus some other trait or characteristic. Since I do not usually identify strongly with only one race, I do not expect others to judge me simply on a race or the fact that I am multiracial, but it is possible they still do. Unfortunately, this is not the case for all multiracial individuals, as this study points out, particularly for those who have experienced blatant discrimination because of the way others perceive their racial background.

Chapter 4
Assimilation versus Overcompensation

*A**ssimilation* is defined as "the act or process of assimilating, or of absorbing information, experiences."[34] As such, *cultural assimilation* is the process by which a minority group is absorbed into a larger, more dominant culture. Countless forms of cultural assimilation exist: getting rid of an accent from a foreign country, changing one's wardrobe to what is considered traditionally "American," and exclusively watching American entertainment and pop culture. In my personal experience living in the American South, individuals who are racially ambiguous and can "pass for White" tend to fall into White culture versus identifying with their minority roots. It is the tendency for those of different ethnic heritage to assimilate to the dominant culture of American society rather than the different non-White cultures that may be part of their blood. The dominant culture in the American South is White culture. Those who openly express their non-White culture are typically labeled as only identifying as one race. Based on personal experience and in conversations with those who are also of mixed race, multiracial people therefore tend to absorb the dominant culture of the American South, which is White culture.

Acculturation is defined as "the process of sharing and learning the cultural traits or social patterns of another group."[35] This is a less extreme version of assimilation because the less dominant culture does not completely absorb the information and experiences from the dominant culture but, instead, simply shares and learns such information and experiences. Oftentimes, when an individual is clearly one race, acculturation is much more common, and that person has one clear culture to share. If that individual is observing a culture apart from their own single culture, then they also have an entirely different culture from which to learn new cultural traits or patterns. This encourages acculturation instead of complete cultural assimilation.

America is what it is today because of acculturation, as immigrants from countries all over the world migrated to America, shared their cultures, and we now have a marvelous melting pot of all different types of cultures throughout the nation. Assimilation, however, has been recognized as a valuable asset in obtaining the best education and, as such, better health, wealth, and social status versus those who do not assimilate completely. For example, the assumption that, when individuals were first coming to America in order to "make it" economically and socially in this country, immigrants needed to assimilate and "become American" to overcome any deficits, including language, culture, dress, and aesthetics generally. The process of assimilation for immigrants has generally always been seen as a positive for one's self and for future generations of one's family.[36] As with anything in life, there are pros and cons to assimilation, but I can say it has certainly impacted how I look at myself and others in American society.

While I am not a first-generation immigrant, my mom did emigrate here from the Philippines, and she assimilated into American culture very quickly. She married my dad, who is White. Upon moving to the United States, she recognized the importance of her future children assimilating into American culture, including receiving a great education and paving our own paths to the "American dream." She became a doctor during a time when women were the minority population as medical doctors. She inspired me to achieve anything and be everything I could possibly be. Since I was not very good at science in high school, I decided early on that being a doctor was not in the cards for me. However, my mother's achievements, experiences, and influence definitely had a hand in my decision to major in political science in college. And as I dived deeper into not only the American political system but also the political systems of other countries, it became clear to me that the law and politics were something in which I loved to immerse myself. As such, I started law school at Charlotte School of Law in the fall of 2012 with one goal in mind: climb to the top of my class.

To achieve this goal, I was a complete "gunner," meaning I was shamelessly a teacher's pet, sat front and center in every class, took notes of every single thing said in class, had a color-coded highlighter system while reading and outlining cases, made meetings with professors during their office hours to get as much face time as possible, took every opportunity to volunteer to help, and never missed a class. I immersed myself, and my identity, in this pursuit.

I finished my first year of law school number one in my class out of about five hundred students—the largest class in Charlotte Law's history. I landed an internship at a large company, and my main focus was helping in the employment law division of the company's legal department. Since this was a company, it was usually the defendant in charges and lawsuits that involved employment discrimination. This was assimilation at its finest.

Throughout the remainder of law school, I became involved in as many student organizations as I possibly could because this was what Elle Woods would have done. Due to the lack of Asian American population, my law school did not have an Asian American organization; however, there was a Black Law Students Association, which was very popular. Not only did I join organizations, but I was also determined to be a leader in every single organization in which I became involved. I was elected to the executive board of every honors society imaginable, including Law Review which is considered one of the most prestigious organizations one can be a part of in law school. I won awards. I achieved a full ride through an academic scholarship. By the end of law school, I was class-elected speaker at graduation and the elected law school representative for the American Bar Association, which meant I got to travel to conferences throughout the country representing Charlotte School of Law. These conferences were somewhat more diverse than what was typically seen in the South but still majority White and still within my comfort zone. I had created my entire identity in my law school accomplishments.

I loved my law school life. I had my friends, most of whom were White. I had my parents and grandmother in Charlotte whom I went to visit occasionally when I could force a break from studying. I had my professors, most of whom again were White. I had my internship at a large corporation, where most attorneys were White. During my last year of law school, I landed a desirable externship in the chambers of the chief district court judge at the federal courthouse. The majority of judges, staff, and other externs at the federal courthouse were White.

Everything seemed to be aligning. I was still, at this point, not concerned about my racial identity, as I was creating my identity through my work in school and felt very at home in the White community. Some would say I was assimilating extremely well, almost to the point of overcompensating. However, there always seemed to be a void when it came to racial identity; feeling like I was not being true to myself while living in the South, like I was throwing a part of my identity away by failing to acknowledge it. I never expressed this to my mom or my brother because I didn't want to admit to them that, during all this, while I was assimilating and overcompensating, I had forgotten about the part of me I never came face-to-face with. I can now say I regret not fully exploring or seeking to learn more about my Filipino heritage and, instead, pushed full steam ahead to White American assimilation as fast as I possibly could. I likely did this because society and the community in which I grew up encouraged "fitting in" to White culture as much as possible. In addition, since my brother did not move to the South with my parents and me, I did not think he would understand where I was coming from, and I was worried he might think I was a "traitor" of our Filipino heritage. We did not discuss this at all while I was growing up.

The feelings can be described as guilt and regret, mostly for the shame I had for the side of myself I had not come to embrace. I had achieved everything possible, and Elle Woods would have been proud. Still, the feeling of something missing wouldn't go away.

After law school, I took and passed the North Carolina bar exam. Shortly thereafter, I started working at a small firm doing business and entertainment law. While working at this firm, I had the unique opportunity to go to court on a fairly regular basis— once or twice per week, depending on the caseload. I was lucky enough to be going to court several times a week for civil cases in state district and superior court. When in court, most of the judges and other attorneys were White.

Ultimately, I ended up leaving the firm and took a job at the large corporation where I had previously interned during law school. I enjoyed the employment discrimination defense work, which was what I did for the following two years there. After that, I took a job as corporate counsel for another company, not as large, but this was part of the appeal of transitioning to this job. I would have the ability to make more of an impact as legal counsel because of the size of the company. Sometimes, I feel I try to find my identity in my profession rather than who I am as a person. I believe part of this stems from my lack of solid racial identity and others' perception of my racial identity throughout life.

Chapter 5
More Elephants

In August of 2017, after only eleven years of operating, my law school shut down. This was devastating for me. I had seen myself as a trailblazer at this relatively new law school, having created a legacy for myself in a city I absolutely loved and called home ... and it just got shut down. As heartbreaking as this was at the time, it was not a total surprise and had been in the making for several months prior. Another identity I had created for myself (via my law school) had completely disappeared, almost overnight.

For a law school, Charlotte School of Law was young when I applied in 2012; it had only been open for about six years. While applying, I knew I wanted to be back in Charlotte, a city I loved, and near my family and friends. When I was accepted with almost a full ride based on my LSAT score, I was ecstatic. I did not commit to attending right away, but deep down, I knew I wanted to start my law journey in Charlotte. I had a lot of internal struggles committing to attend a law school that was so new because I did not want anyone to have any reason to question the legitimacy of my degree or intelligence. Ultimately, I saw going to a new law school as a challenge to be a pioneer of a school yet to be well-known, and I wanted to pave the way for those who came after me by being a great attorney, thus representing the school in the best possible light I could. Also, law school was expensive, and the scholarship was a hefty amount—extremely hard to turn down. I knew it would be a challenge going in, but I was excited for the journey and to create my own brand, knowing I could not rely on the name of my school to open doors for me; I had to do it myself.

Around the time I began attending classes, people started to question the number of students attending the law school (i.e., taking out student loans) versus how many graduates were actually passing the bar exam. In short, the American Bar Association determined the school was not providing adequate education to the number of students it was taking in. This was a direct blow to me. Even though the school was fully and legitimately accredited while I attended, and I passed the bar exam on the first try (the same bar exam people from every other law school in the state had taken), the shutdown happening a short two years after I graduated made me feel as though my degree was worthless. I had gained part of my identity from my school and then my professional career; the two were intertwined, as many lawyers may tell you. I have noticed that lawyers—more so than most any other profession, for some reason—put a great deal of value in where they went to school.

When you sit down at a table of lawyers you have just met, and you look like me (a young, mixed-race female), one of the first questions that inevitably comes up is, "So, where did you go to law school?" This question is yet another way to place someone in a "box," to characterize a person based on one sliver of their whole being. I was always insecure in talking about where I went to law school, even while in law school, because my school was still new, was for profit, and had not yet proven itself, but at least while I was there, I could list off all the student organizations in which I was involved and led and could talk about how great I was doing in school. After law school, people don't really care if you were a representative of the ABA Law School Division, or on the executive board of Law Review, or the class-elected speaker. This question had already been somewhat awkward to answer when the school was open; now this question became an even bigger elephant in the room since the law school completely shut down.

This experience was comparable to my experience of the racial identity question because there's simply not a one- or two-word answer I can give in either situation without also providing further explanation. Both became exhausting to have to talk about and constantly explain. And as I look back, having to explain what I am racially comprised of has been a lifelong exhaustion.

Exacerbating the law school situation, I was also experiencing something many young female attorneys encounter, which is sexism as a legal professional. This typically did not come from other attorneys but usually those who were non-lawyers. For example, during my first year of practice, sometimes when at the courthouse, the court clerk would ask me where the attorney was. I was right there in front of him. Other times, if I met someone in a social setting and was asked what I do for a living, if I answered with, "I'm a lawyer," I have actually been corrected by a stranger stating to me, "Oh, you mean you're a paralegal?" As absurd as that statement seems, it has, in fact, happened to me more than once.

The main takeaways from my law school shutdown were twofold: 1) I was glad I already had experience navigating awkward questions and conversations with new people about my race, which I could apply to law school since an explanation was usually required after my initial answer, and 2) I did not have to draw my identity from a school, profession, or race. It only took a devastating shutdown of my former law school—a school and community I had put my heart and soul into—in order to make these realizations.

Chapter 6
Mixed Up in the Media

There are millions of characters in mainstream media, movies, and televisions shows. Most of these characters generally pass as one race that is obvious to the audience. How many multiracial or racially ambiguous characters can you think of off the top of your head? Probably not many. You may see this changing as Hollywood champions—or, at the very least, pays lip service to—supporting racial diversity. In the meantime, however, there are celebrities of mixed race, or who are racially ambiguous, who have experienced similar feelings to those of us mixed-race or racially ambiguous "civilians." These celebrities have spoken out about their own identity crises and the lack of representation of mixed-race individuals in mainstream media.

Hollywood actress Shay Mitchell was the focus of a *New York Post* Page Six article in 2015 entitled, "Shay Mitchell Tried to Hide Her Filipino Heritage as a Teen." The article discusses how Mitchell grew up in a suburb of predominantly White Toronto and, because of the lack of representation of anyone else who looked like her, would frequently dye her hair, wear colored contacts, and avoid the sun to stay as pale as possible.[37]

I remember devouring this story because Mitchell and I had very similar experiences. I did not avoid the sun like she did, but I did attempt to fit in by changing my physical features as a teen. In 2018, Mitchell further opened up to *Elite Daily* in an article entitled "Shay Mitchell Shared Her Heartbreaking Struggles with the Lack of Asian Representation in Beauty," in which she confessed that when she was a teenager, she wanted to be something she wasn't, as she was seeking to fit in and resemble a White girl and not acknowledge the part of her that was Filipino. She admitted that looking back at the times where she felt she did not meet the beauty "norms" as represented in the media was her biggest beauty mistake. Mitchell encouraged women of all races, particularly Asian girls, to celebrate their own unique looks.[38]

For me, growing up, there were certainly times when I wanted to be something represented in the media as "beautiful," something I did not fit into. Fortunately, I have since learned to embrace my own physical appearance and appreciate physical attributes different than what society once held as the highest standard of "beauty."

In 2016, actress Meghan Markle became a topic of regular media news as she was publicly dating Prince Harry before ultimately marrying him in 2017. Around this time, I read multiple articles in various newspapers and magazines about Markle speaking out about her racial ambiguity. Markle's father is White, and her mother is Black. One article informed readers that Markle's mother was dark-skinned, whereas Markle was a light-skinned baby, and when her mother used to walk her around the White suburbs of Los Angeles, people used to assume Markle's mother was the nanny and ask where Markle's mother was.[39] This part of the article reminded me of a story my parents used to tell me. One day when I was a baby, and my dad was walking with my Uncle Stephen and me—with my dark hair and dark eyes—in the stroller, an elderly White woman said to him, "She's beautiful. Where did she come from?" To which my dad responded, "She is my daughter."

In the moment, my dad did not think much of it, but when he looks back on it, he does not even know what the woman meant by, "Where did she come from?" without any additional context. My dad now believes this had something to do with my multiracial heritage, particularly since the question came from an older, White woman.

My mom heard the story when my dad got home and immediately thought it was an odd question ... and still does. My mom believes the elderly woman was stereotyping, that she did not think it was possible a White man with blond hair and blue eyes could have a baby with dark hair and dark eyes. Today, we laugh about the story, but it was certainly a memorable moment and still makes us think. There are certain comments made in life that may be fleeting to someone else but actually make an impact on others—this being one of them.

Markle also mentioned in the article that, based on what makeup or wardrobe she wore to an audition in Hollywood, she could come off as whatever race she pleased—Latina, African American— however, she quickly realized she was never "ethnic enough" due to her racial ambiguity. This posed challenges for her to land certain roles in show business, until her big break playing Rachel Zane on *Suits*, in which she described her character as "the Goldilocks of [her] acting career—where [she] finally was just right."[40] Markle acknowledged that this "Goldilocks" moment was a rarity in show business.

I also encountered issues of not being "ethnic enough." For example, in middle school, I once auditioned for a commercial, and the main character was an Asian girl. When I started speaking, the casting director asked which role I was vying for. I informed her I was there to read for the main character. After the audition, the casting director informed me my audition went well, but if she was being honest, I did "not look Asian enough" to meet the standard they were seeking. Other than the way I looked—racially ambiguous—I am sure my voice, which consists of a somewhat valley girl accent, did not help me seem any more "Asian" in the eyes of the casting decision maker. I do not recall what was the product or service being advertised in the commercial, but I do know it was nothing specifically targeted toward Asian people. Experiences such as this one made it difficult to identify with one racial group and further made me feel like a "traitor" in trying to identify with the Filipino side of my race.

The Markle article discussed how she was subject to hurtful comments and personal attacks regarding her race once people found out she and Prince Harry were dating, getting married, and everything thereafter. Markle said, "I decided to carve my own path [...] you create the identity you want for yourself, just as my ancestors did when they were given their freedom."[41]

This was certainly relatable to me in light of my inability to clearly identify with one particular race and my inherent quest for acceptance.

In July 2017, the popular women's magazine *Elle* published an article entitled, "Meghan Markle Opens Up about 'Ethnically Ambiguous' Childhood." A quote that resonated with me from this article was, "My hope is for the world to get to a place where it's colour blind. [...] While my mixed heritage may have created a grey area surrounding my self-identification, keeping me with a foot on both sides of the fence, I have come to embrace that."[42]

This was an important statement for me to read and relate to, especially in light of the high profile she achieved after marrying Prince Harry, the then-prince of the British monarchy—a historically White institution. Self-identification problems for mixed-race individuals is not a topic that had previously been brought into the conversation for anyone associated with the British monarchy. Markle's vulnerable discussion of this topic gave me hope that she would bring perspective to people who have never thought about the identity crisis a mixed-race person can (and usually does) feel.

In an article entitled, "Chrissy Teigen Was Once Embarrassed by Her Ethnic Culture," supermodel Chrissy Teigen discussed being raised by a Thai mother and Norwegian American father. When discussing her children, she expands the discussion from cuisine to racial identification generally:

> Teigen credits that complex about her culture to ignorance and a desire to fit in, things she's since overcome. Now, as a mom to two-year-old daughter Luna and a not-yet-born baby boy, Teigen is aware of the importance of racial representation and diversity, especially for children. This is why, instead of "blond Barbies," Teigen gives Luna brown-skinned dolls—which they've named Coco Babies—who look like Luna. She also puts on children's TV and movies that feature racially diverse characters whom Luna can see herself in. "Having something that represents them or looks a little like them, it changes everything," Teigen says. "I never thought that way before. I always thought, 'Why can't she just play with a regular blond Barbie?' There is something to be said about having something that has your skin color, your hair color, your eye color, your eye shape."[43]

I grew up playing with Barbies and was never bothered with the fact that the traditional Barbie had blond hair and blue eyes; however, when I first saw Barbies in the toy store with brown hair, brown eyes, and tan skin—like me—I remember feeling a sense of excitement, as if the toy store made this Barbie doll just for me. Other than changing her hair color, eye color, and skin color, nothing else was different about this Barbie. Even still, I felt I could more relate to this doll simply because of the way she looked.

Teigen understands the complications of being a racially ambiguous child in a world that wants only certainty. Teigen's interviewer observed:

> Having grown up multiracial and not knowing where exactly she fit in, Teigen worries that Luna—whose father and Teigen's husband, John Legend, is Black—might face a similar complex. Though, with the world's fast-changing racial landscape, she hopes things will be different for her kids as they grow up. "I remember

feeling confused when I grew up, filling out the forms on those standardized tests. I was like, 'Am I Pacific Islander? What am I? I don't even know!'" Teigen says. "And then there was 'Other.' But I always said 'Asian' for some wild reason, even though it's a perfect fifty-fifty. Still, I remember the biggest question growing up was, 'What are you? What are you? What are you?' And you're like, 'Oh, my God.' I worry sometimes Luna is going to be so much in the middle that she's not going to know, but I think by the time she grows up, it's such a melting pot, this whole world now."[44]

Multiracial individuals who have children—who will inevitably be multiracial by nature of at least one parent being multiracial—understand the identity dilemmas and confusion their children will face. I hope these parents can speak openly about these challenges with their children to ensure their children know they are not alone. Multiracial parents are critical in helping their multiracial children navigate their feelings on this complex topic (including which "box" to check on standardized tests). While I did not have conversations on this topic with my parents growing up because I never thought to bring it up with them, I know they would have looked into resources on how to help me navigate the feelings of confusion and guilt I often had.

In a *NBC News* article from February 2021 entitled, "'What Are You?' How Multiracial Americans Respond and How It's Changing," the author acknowledged that:

[S]ome of the more recent focus on people of mixed-Asian American Pacific Islander heritage has been thanks to Vice President Kamala Harris, whose mother and father emigrated to the US from India and Jamaica, respectively, and who has openly discussed how both parts of her identity have shaped her as a person and a public official. [...] [A]s Asians have gained prominence in American society, so have those of mixed-Asian heritage in other areas of public life. Tennis phenomenon Naomi Osaka is of Japanese and Black heritage. Millions hang on every word of model and author Chrissy Teigen, who is of Thai and European descent. DC blockbuster Aquaman has grossed more than $1 billion with a cast led by Jason Momoa, who's part Native Hawaiian and part White. Musical success stories range from Bruno Mars (part Filipino) to Ne-Yo (part Chinese) to Karen O of the Yeah Yeah Yeahs (part Korean). The list goes on and on. It wasn't always that way—or at least, it wasn't so openly discussed.[45]

While the number of mixed-heritage celebrities in the public eye is rising, this is still a new phenomenon that is not discussed nearly enough. High-profile, mixed-race public figures in the media are still few and far between.

A February 2016 report published from the University of Southern California Annenberg entitled, "The Comprehensive Annenberg Report on Diversity in Entertainment" found that in "2015's Hollywood film, TV programs, and digital series [...] while women are increasingly included as writers, creators, and directors in television, racial and ethnic minorities remain mostly excluded from every realm of television and film."[46] The CARD report concluded that Hollywood "still functions as a straight, White boy's club," where women and ethnic and racial minorities need not apply for jobs.[47] The report notes that audiences, actors, creators, and executives of color in the entertainment industries remain defined by exclusion from the industry and lack of visibility on the movie screen.

Additionally, an article entitled, "#OscarsSoWhite: How Stuart Hall Explains Why Nothing Changes in Hollywood and Everything Is Changing" demonstrates the main problem with Hollywood and its version of representation. Through the studies of Stuart Hall, it explains Hall's writings on ideology, representation, and hegemony to build a theoretical framework for studying: 1) Hollywood's historical ethnic, racial, and gender homogeneity; 2) competing public discourses surrounding diversity in Hollywood; and 3) the digital turn in the structure and content of Hollywood.[48]

Hall's work significantly contributed to the development of a cultural studies cannon on media representations, audiences, and ethnic and racial differences. In particular, Hall conceptualized cultural representations as a complex set of production and interpretative practices informed by a society's norms and values and, thereby, imbued with social meaning. Thus, Hollywood, as a globally dominant producer and purveyor of cultural representations, is a significant site for studying contemporary contestations over ethnic, racial, and gender differences and how those conflicts speak to changes in broader relationships of power. Throughout his scholarship, Hall foregrounded the political significance of studying media representations of differences generally and ethnic, racial, and class differences specifically.

Hall is quoted in the article as saying, "What cultural studies has helped me to understand is that the media plays a part in the formation, in the constitution, of the things they reflect. It is not that there is a world outside, 'out there,' which exists free of the discourses of representations. What is 'out there' is, in part, constituted by how it is represented."[49]

This goes along with the identity crisis I suffered as a child when I did not see many people in movies or television who looked like me. I did not think anyone in the world was experiencing the same identity crisis I was constantly facing internally. The media is supposed to be a reflection of what is out in the world; however, the world also attempts to reflect what it sees in mainstream media.

The article goes on to explain the irony between Hollywood seeking to represent diversity but still lacking diversity in those who are responsible for creating and publishing the content—film and TV production:

> Although network TV depictions of ethnic and racial minorities are incrementally improving, executive decision-making and content production remain constrained by the racial and gender power structures in Hollywood. It is that privilege that is under contestation in the Hollywood paradox—the lack of diversity

in film and TV production yet TV's increasing shift toward on-screen representational diversity. However, the focus by news media and cultural activists on improving on-screen diversity shifts attention away from a critique of institutional power. As Gray (2013) argues, the focus on the representational relieves pressure from the need to change economic, employment, and labor practices. In that sense, conflicts over the lack of diversity in Hollywood are indicative of broader social conflicts over the changing status of ethnicity, race, and gender in the US.[50]

This shows that the issue is much deeper than merely casting "diverse" individuals in main character and supporting roles in movies and television. It is important those same "diverse" perspectives are considered and included when filming and producing the media to ensure the perspective is accurately depicted. From my perspective as a mixed-race individual, it would mean much more to me having a character on-screen who understood the trials, tribulations, and triumphs of being multiracial instead of merely having someone who looked similar to me.

Another article from the *Journal of Ethnic and Migration Studies* discussed a variety of issues surrounding multiracial experiences and proposed a framework where mixedness can be better understood globally. The article stated that one of the main issues is a lack of representation in Hollywood:

[A] strange trend that has been happening in media has been the use of multiracial identities to cast White actors or using multiracial individuals to cast characters who are ethnically monoracial [...] only multiracial characters should be played by only multiracial individuals and vice versa, but there's definitely a deflating feeling when you get excited about seeing a character similar to you but are disappointed to not see an actor who represents that identity. [...] [T]his is a complicated and ongoing discussion among multiracial individuals, and there's no right or wrong answer but something to think about. Hollywood has

never had a great track record in terms of casting appropriately—
especially for people of color. Overall, there are not enough BIPOC
or multiracial roles to go around in the first place, and I do not
blame actors of color for taking what they can get.[51]

Every girl growing up in the 1990s understood the importance
of identifying with a Disney princess since the "classic" Disney
movies were a huge part of childhood entertainment and, for
children growing up in this era, a huge part of life, as this was
what we expected life to be like. (The unrealistic Disney princess
romance expectation is an entirely different topic for another day or
book.) Growing up, most of the "original" Disney princesses were
White, with the exception of a few, such as Jasmine, Pocahontas,
and Mulan. Notably, of these three, only Jasmine is canonically
a princess. Even the Disney princesses who were "diverse" still
appeared to be assimilated into American culture. They had the
body type, hair, face, and accent as any other White Disney princess.
Looking back, the only things different from the White and
"diverse" Disney princesses were their skin color and wardrobe.
Since the time I was growing up watching Disney movies, it appears
Disney princesses have become more diverse, like the addition of
Tiana in the *Princess and the Frog* to Mirabel in *Encanto* to Raya in
Raya and the Last Dragon, but not necessarily racially ambiguous.
Even with the addition of more Disney princesses, there is not
one whom I feel I could totally identify with if I were a child in
today's world.

For girls growing up in the 1990s, almost as important as
identifying with a Disney princess was the importance of identifying
with a Spice Girl. The Spice Girls were a British pop girl group
formed in 1994, comprised of Melanie Brown, also known as Mel
B (Scary Spice), Melanie Chisholm or Mel C (Sporty Spice), Emma
Bunton (Baby Spice), Geri Halliwell (Ginger Spice), and Victoria
Beckham (Posh Spice). I believe one of the primary appeals of the
Spice Girls was the fact that they represented a diverse group of
women—Black, White with blond hair, White with red hair, a girl's

girl, and a tomboy. For me, a mixed-race girl growing up in the 1990s, I was happy to see such a diverse group of beautiful and talented women; however, I still could not identify with just one. This is just another example of the media influence on racially ambiguous individuals and their inability to feel like they fit in anywhere. The Spice Girl I ultimately ended up identifying with most, and dressed up as on multiple occasions, was Ginger Spice because I fell in love with her voice and personality from music videos and the media. I ended up relating to her based on her media personality rather than her outside appearance.

In 2019, I remember watching a talk show and seeing actress America Ferrera appear on the show, promoting her new book *American Like Me*. She talked about her Honduran heritage and her ability to maintain her parents' culture while also assimilating into American culture. Ferrera's book explores the importance of identity in America through interviews with various individuals in several different fields of work and entertainment. Specifically, she interviewed thirty-one of her friends, peers, and heroes to share their stories about life between cultures. She spoke with actors, comedians, athletes, politicians, artists, and writers. Every single one of them had personal, deep connections to more than one culture, whether they were immigrants, second or third generations of immigrants, or indigenous people. "[E]ach of them struggled to establish a sense of self, find belonging, and feel seen. And they call themselves 'American' enthusiastically, reluctantly, or not at all."[52]

Ferrera's book really resonated with me. I found it to be heartwarming, interesting, and it inspired me to think more often and more deeply about the issue of racial ambiguity and its intersection with the human need for identity. It also forced me to think about those in my life who may be experiencing the same thing but also not really ever speaking about it or acknowledging the unique opportunity and dilemma.

Chapter 7
Personally

Growing up, most of my friends did not look like me. I had friends of different races, ethnicities, and nationalities. What's the difference between these different terms? They are frequently interchanged, so I thought it would be helpful to define them here.

Race is defined as "physical characteristics that define a person as being a member of a specific group." Examples include "skin color, hair color and texture, eye color, facial features, physical build."[53]

Ethnicity is defined as "cultural characteristics that define a person as being a member of a specific group." Examples include "language, accent, religion, styles of dress, hairstyles, social customs, food and dietary preferences or restrictions."[54]

Nationality is defined as "the legal sense of belonging to a specific political nation state." An example is citizenship, either by birthright or naturalization.[55]

People will frequently ask, "What are you?" And when I ask for clarification, they then inquire, "Like, what's your nationality?" Well, my nationality is American, as I was born and raised in the

United States of America. Race and ethnicity are the questions I have more difficulty answering because there are many different races and ethnicities of which I am comprised.

When others are trying to relate to you or put you in a certain "box" to define you by certain stereotypes, having a one-word answer to these questions makes that easier. I have found that when I tell someone the mixture of races and ethnicities of which I am comprised, they typically prefer to define me in the one most easy to remember and most unique, which is usually Filipino. I have no qualms with this, but individuals must start to accept that as America continues evolving into the melting pot it prides itself on being, we must stop attempting to define individuals by racial or ethnic stereotypes.

I reached out to some people in my personal life whom I have been able to identify as also having experiences with racial ambiguity. I knew the people I reached out to would have interesting perspectives to share. Prior to these conversations, I had never had in-depth discussions about racial ambiguity or being a mixed-race individual with these people—many of whom I have known for several years. I blame this on the fact that the topic of a multiracial individual's struggle with identity is not openly talked about very often. It is a vulnerable and uncomfortable perspective to share.

Priscilla

In elementary and middle school, I had a couple of friends who were also mixed races. One of these friends is Priscilla, who is Filipino and Hispanic. Like me, many people could not tell upon meeting her exactly what race or ethnicity she was—and rightfully so, as she was a beautiful kaleidoscope of a few different races. Priscilla and I always got along with everyone and never felt left out because we did not look exactly like our White counterparts. Growing up in the same neighborhood and going to the same elementary and middle school, we had very similar perspectives of ourselves and how we fit into the world as multiracial children. The topic of race never really came up between Priscilla and me, nor do I recall anyone we went to school with asking us about our respective races. Priscilla came from a family with different ethnicities, making her search for her roots equally as confusing. Did she have to choose a side? Which side did she feel more comfortable with and relate to more? It was a conundrum we both experienced but never really fully addressed with each other ... until now. I had the chance to listen to my childhood friend's perspective on this very topic.

Me: What is your racial makeup?

Priscilla: I am Mexican and Filipino.

Me: Do people frequently ask you the question, "What are you?"

Priscilla: All. The. Time. Whether it's an Uber driver, someone at the grocery checkout line, a person I just met, it seems this question follows me everywhere.

Me: Does this bother you (in the past or currently)?

Priscilla: I love that this question asks about the past and currently because I have had different feelings about it. Growing up, this question didn't bother me. I would also say I wasn't fully aware of how race and microaggressions came into play in my life until later. [...] Nowadays, I very much loathe being asked this question for a few reasons:

1. It is not uncommon for someone to say, "That's why you are so pretty!" after I answer this question. I am not in need of any more microaggressions and fetishizing based on my looks.

2. Why is my race a topic of conversation? Or an icebreaker? I will never forget being at a gathering at a friend's house in the kitchen with mostly people I had not met before. Someone I knew said, "Priscilla, you're Mexican, right? That's why you're so feisty!" All the eyes turned to look at me, and I was painfully aware I was the only person of color in this room. It's one thing to feel "othered" via forms that don't give you a "mixed-race box" to check, but it's another to feel othered in person.

3. The "What are you?" definitely triggers me more than someone asking, "Where are you from?" It is unusual for White people to be asked either of these questions. The caveat to all this is if someone who is BIPOC asks me where I'm from, as I know we have had shared experiences.

Me: Have you ever felt pressure to "choose" a certain race with which to primarily identify?

Priscilla: I personally struggle more with feeling like I don't actually belong in the races I identify with. A big part of this is that I am not fluent in neither Spanish nor Tagalog and have had my race dismissed as a result. I traveled to Mexico for a bachelorette party and was frequently approached to translate for my group as I am mostly Mexican presenting. I was asked, "What's wrong with you?" multiple times when I told people I didn't speak Spanish. I have been at *Simbang Gabi*, a Filipino Christmas tradition with mass followed by food, and had *titas* tell me I'm not Filipino while my mother, who was born in Manila, sat a few tables away. The impostor syndrome is strong in feeling that I am not Mexican enough for the Mexicans, Filipino enough for the Filipinos, or American enough for Americans. I continue to work to dismantle this thinking, but it's quite difficult.

Me: What is a specific experience that you recall (if any) where you felt like you had to "choose" a side when it came to your race or ethnicity? What was your feeling and response to this situation?

Priscilla: I don't feel that I've experienced this per se. I will say that I grew up surrounded by my mom's Filipino side of the family and have been pretty removed from my dad's Mexican side due to complexities within the family. I may feel more Filipino in the sense that I grew up around relatives, eating the food, learning about the culture. Again, this is complicated due to the fact that I am mostly Mexican presenting.

Me: Based on your own experiences, what or who do you feel creates this type of pressure for multiracial individuals?

Priscilla: From a beauty standpoint, I feel the difficulty for people who are multiracial is to fit into the "boxes" of what Western/

Eurocentric beauty standards are, as they generally celebrate Whiteness from the shape of your nose to the size of your hips. These beauty standards were not made by us or for us. You see the effect of this to a great extent in Asian countries where celebrities are fairer in skin color, and skin-lightening products are an $8 billion industry (as of 2020) and growing. It has been incredible to see more people reclaim their beauty and bodies in more recent years.

Alexis

Alexis is a dear friend of mine from college and law school. We met because we lived in the same dorm and had many of the same classes freshman year of college. When I first met her, I remember thinking she was strikingly beautiful (and still is!), and everyone else seemed to notice her extremely rare beauty too. Come to find out, she had won many beauty pageant titles, which completely made sense. Make no mistake, though, there is much more to Alexis than just her beauty—she is one of the most intelligent, driven, and compassionate human beings I know to exist in this world. We often joke about how, when we first met, we both had "resting bitch face," and both of us thought we hated each other initially— for no reason other than the fact that we did not seem thrilled to meet each other. Very soon after our first encounter, however, we became close friends.

In college, we sometimes had conversations about how we looked very different compared to our college counterparts at UNC-W(hite). We lived in the same dorm and would study and go out together, along with other students in our dorm. We also became very close during our first year of law school. But we never got very deep into the conversation surrounding our multiracial backgrounds and racial ambiguity. Alexis has a much different perspective than I do, as she spent a great deal of her childhood growing up in Charlotte as a mixed kid. I always wondered if she also encountered struggles identifying with her roots. Again, this was not something that was openly and fully discussed between us until now.

Me: What is your racial makeup?

Alexis: Half Puerto Rican and half African American.

Me: Do people frequently ask you the question, "What are you?"

Alexis: People have asked me this question ever since I can remember. I remember being very confused at a young age. I remember thinking the answer should be something like, "I'm a girl; I'm a child." One of my first memories is another kid coming up to me and saying, "You're yellow." I was very confused. The only way I knew how to come back at that was, "I'm orange, not yellow." When I got home from school, I told my mom about this conversation, and she was not thrilled to hear about it. My mom is an African American woman. She would tell stories about how people used to joke with her that she stole me, or they gave her the wrong baby in the hospital. This bothered her, but it also bothered me because it was due to these stories [that] I started to realize the difference between my mom and me: I didn't really look like her. Other people would notice it too. At a young age, people brought it to my attention, and then I started to think about it myself.

Me: Does this bother you (in the past or currently)?

Alexis: As a child, it confused me. [...] It bothered me in the sense that it was something other people felt like they had to call out—I didn't see anything different. Most of what bothered me was why they were asking. For example, when I tell people my racial makeup, some would respond with, "Oh, you're so well-spoken." I interpreted this to mean that the fact that I am well-spoken doesn't match up with what that person assumed about me from what they saw. Sometimes I would interpret the question of "What are you?" as someone asking because they weren't anticipating that I could be the race(s) they think I might be. That would make me upset—I would think things like, *How dare you? And how dare you ask me in order to validate your own assumption?* Now, it doesn't really bother me anymore because I understand the root of the question, and I think of it as a teachable moment (if I have time for that). But in my youth, it definitely bothered me.

Me: Have you ever felt pressure to "choose" a certain race with which to primarily identify?

Alexis: Yes, all the time. It was always a juxtaposition between being so unique that what you "are" is being discussed but then so overlooked at the same time because there wasn't a space to understand that uniqueness yet. I felt like a unicorn—like this is such a big deal, but no one is hearing me—I'm not one or the other. I felt zoomed in on but overlooked at the same time. It was also frustrating having to teach other people about this simply because you are different.

Me: What is a specific experience you recall (if any) where you felt like you had to "choose" a side when it came to your race or ethnicity? What was your feeling and response to this situation?

Alexis: I remember End-Of-Grade tests in elementary school, where they would ask for my race, and back then, I couldn't pick "other" or "two or more races." I had to choose only one race. Now, there are more options, and it is much better. But I remember crying one time because I thought I would choose the wrong answer, it would affect my grade, or it would upset my parents because I was choosing to align with one side or another. I was having to "choose" [what] I couldn't choose. Additionally, there were times when I've said to [people] in the Black community, "I'm Puerto Rican and Black," and they would respond with, "Okay, so you're Black." This likely stems from the fact that many Puerto Ricans have roots in Africa; however, my Spanish side comes from the Canary Islands of Spain, so they don't have that past African root most Puerto Ricans have. I have also had people tell me to "go by what your dad is." My dad is Puerto Rican, but my mom is Black. Failing to acknowledge my mom's side of the family, who originated as slaves in South Carolina, is not proper. I am both. One of the reasons I moved to the Bronx this past year is I wanted to live within the Spanish community. I wanted to be as close as I could to my dad's side of the family's first experience in America, which was New York City—specifically, the Bronx. As a mixed person, I have this beautiful, kinky, curly hair, but where I grew up, a lot of Black women didn't wear their hair naturally. I previously never wore it natural, but I do now. I wanted to be able to wear my hair [naturally, in the way it was when I was born] to the point where I'm not manipulating it, [where] I don't recognize my hair texture. I went through an identity crisis when I started wearing my hair naturally—mostly because I've now seen myself in a way I've never seen myself before. I have now finally really started to embrace my natural hair and see the beauty in it. I also couldn't believe I hadn't had this connection with myself previously. This topic of being a mixed individual is interesting and has come up in so many different ways throughout my life.

Me: Based on your own experiences, what or who do you feel creates this type of pressure for multiracial individuals?

Alexis: It is deep … none of us were around when it started. We are just a by-product of the pressure created for multiracial individuals. America has such a fractured past with race and how people have been treated in this country. In America, race has historically been focused on in negative ways. It's almost like all you see reported are the negative stereotypes and negative things about race. It's only negative things we see constantly. Everyone's been taught this standard of Whiteness, that everyone, as society, is trying to reach because that's what's been taught. Colonization and demonization of races happened because of control and fear. It's only natural for generations to continue reporting those stereotypes. Unfortunately, I have also seen negativity as it comes to racial fetishization. For example, when I did pageants, I overheard White women who were in the pageants with me talk about my skin color and say they were going to be with a Black man so they could have babies who look like me. The women who said this were the same ones who said if they see a Black man in the street, they would run or cross the street. These comments just never added up for me. As a society, we need to do better.

Courtney

In my sorority at UNC Wilmington, I met a girl during rush by the name of Courtney, who was a junior when I was a freshman. Courtney was, and still is, the life of the party in any room she walks into. When rushing Phi Mu, she immediately stood out as someone I could relate to because I could tell she was a mixed kid too. She was half White and half Korean. She also had a *strong* southern accent, which was what she was known for. From the day I met Courtney, I could tell she did not care at all what anyone thought about her, and I have always admired that about her. Courtney is also gay. She always seemed as though she was completely secure in who she was and never thought twice about how others might perceive her. Courtney's combination of being a gay, half White and half Asian sorority girl in a southern school, with a strong southern accent, definitely made her stand out. I particularly admired Courtney's humor, wit, and storytelling skills. During our first-year retreat as freshman, a few of the older girls took all the new girls to a house about an hour away from campus, where we were all supposed to bond as a class over the weekend. Courtney was one of the five or six older Phi Mu girls who attended the freshman retreat. During the retreat, we had a full itinerary of icebreakers, games, and other planned "forced" fun; in reality, it was all fun but also exhausting by the end of each day. Courtney, however, was able to keep the attention of a group of exhausted girls and enthrall us for hours with her interesting and hilarious stories of being in Phi Mu so far. I vividly remember being extremely ready for bed, but then Courtney would start telling her stories, and somehow, I suddenly had enough energy to stay up until the wee hours of the night—which we all did, just listening to and laughing at Courtney's stories. None of Courtney's stories had to do with her race or sexuality; they simply had to do with her experiences in college thus far and with other Phi Mus (some we knew, and some we didn't know). She encapsulated a person who truly wanted to share her experiences with us younger girls, make light of every situation that may have seemed terrible at the time, and let us know we chose the right group of girls with which to experience this incredible time of our lives called "college." Courtney and I would occasionally discuss our racial ambiguity but not in as much depth as we are now.

Me: What is your racial makeup?

Courtney: White and Korean. My mom's side is very country, and her lineage goes back to some of the first settlers in Virginia. Conversely, my dad moved to America from Korea when he was twelve and could not speak English. Talk about an identity crisis; I'm equally both.

Me: Do people frequently ask you the question, "What are you?"

Courtney: All the time. I was born and raised in a majority White Southern Baptist town in North Carolina. I was the only Asian at my high school in Lexington. My high school was 96 percent White and 4 percent Black; Asians were not even part of the calculation because I was the only one. I just knew I never fit in because I felt so unique and so different.

Me: Does this bother you (in the past or currently)?

Courtney: It does not offend me. People have gotten a little smarter to phrase it as, "Where are you from?" or "What is your heritage?" or "Where do your ethnic features come from?" instead of just, "What are you?" It bothered me when I was a small child because other kids would ask me things like, "Why do you look like that?" "Why are your eyes slanted?" "Are you Chinese?" "Are you Asian or Korean?" As an older kid, teenager, and up until now, the question bothers me a little bit but never much because I attribute the curiosity of this question more to ignorance than racism. I look at this question as an opportunity to educate. There are a lot of people who grew up in the South who have never seen anyone like me before, so I see it as a chance to be a representation of Asians and, for example, educate on the difference between Koreans and other Asians.

Me: Have you ever felt pressure to "choose" a certain race with which to primarily identify?

Courtney: Yes, definitely in high school, I felt like I had to choose White. I had blue contacts and blond highlights. All the girls I grew up with and all the girls in our sorority were mostly White and blond. I definitely felt the pressure to fit in and look like them physically, up until society started to change, and I started to see more Asians on television in college.

Me: What is a specific experience you recall (if any) where you felt like you had to "choose" a side when it came to your race or ethnicity? What was your feeling and response to this situation?

Courtney: Growing up, I felt I had to identify more with my White side, and I chose to be redneck and country because that was how I fit in. Now, I identify more with my Asian side than my White side, but I still speak with a southern accent and engage in activities that are stereotypical of White people like shooting guns, playing golf, playing cornhole, riding four-wheelers, and boating. One thing I liked about living in San Francisco was I never got the question of "What is your heritage?" because it was so much more culturally diverse, particularly with [regard to the] Asian population. When I moved back to North Carolina, I became hyperaware of my Asian side because there were hardly any Asians around at places I would go to. Asians don't accept me because I can't speak Korean. Now, I am this juxtaposition where I don't fit in anywhere, which I've learned to embrace. It took some time for me to accept this because I always wanted to fit in, but now I'm proud of it.

Me: Based on your own experiences, what or who do you feel creates this type of pressure for multiracial individuals?

Courtney: Pressure to fit in with the cool kids. I feel most of my societal pressure stemmed from high school to fit into the majority, which was the White crowd.

Bronwyn

In adulthood, we all know it is more difficult to make friends than in childhood and school. Most friends in adulthood are carried over from some type of schooling or a connection made through a friend group that stemmed from some type of school or community we encountered frequently when we were younger. Other than going to work, adulthood offers very little opportunity for frequent interactions with other adults unless you join some type of group or go out to social settings on a regular basis. In short, it takes much more concerted effort to make social contacts as an adult versus a child or teenager.

One of the most interesting friends I have made during my journey through adulthood is Bronwyn. Much like a "meet-cute" in a romantic comedy, Bronwyn and I met in the elevator of the apartment building in which we both resided at the time. In this fifty-one-story apartment building in uptown Charlotte, residents typically parked on floors one through seven, then took the elevator up to their respective floors. On this day, we had both parked on the second floor, coming home from work. We both waited in the elevator lobby area, watching the TV, which was playing ESPN. Bronwyn looked at me and asked, "Is it just me, or is it only sports that's ever on these TVs?" I laughed and said, "Yeah, that's about right. Yay sports." Bronwyn then talked about how she had just moved there six weeks ago and was just noticing nothing else ever played on common area televisions but sports. I thought it was a good observation, then complimented the bright-yellow sweater she was wearing on a rainy day in the middle of March. When she got off on the fourteenth floor, I still had ten more floors to ride up, but we both expressed how we hoped to see each other again. Having felt like I could be friends with her, I creepily looked her up on the resident portal, then located her on social media and messaged her, asking her, on a "girl date." We ended up going out about a week later and have been good friends ever since.

When I first met Bronwyn, I assumed she was White. But while we were chatting away on our "girl date," she informed me she was a citizen of South Africa, and her ethnicity was White and Korean. I told her I was a mixed kid, too, to which she informed me she could not put a finger on what I was either. We did not speak about this topic for too long, but it was certainly a bonding point, as I had found another person who likely had difficulty answering the "What are you?" line of questioning. Bronwyn and I would occasionally discuss our racial ambiguity but not very in depth. I had the chance to chat with Bronwyn about this topic, and let's just say, it resulted in a tearful, but joyful, conversation.

Me: What is your racial makeup?

Bronwyn: South Korean (Mother has mostly Korean and some Japanese in her heritage) and White South African; Dad is a mix between Dutch and English.

Me: Do people frequently ask you the question, "What are you?"

Bronwyn: ALL THE TIME. When I did a very brief modeling stint, I was in the category "ethnically ambiguous."

Me: Does this bother you (in the past or currently)?

Bronwyn: It did in the past, but I'm learning to be grateful for my uniqueness and the fact that I have more opportunities to relate to others.

Me: Have you ever felt pressure to "choose" a certain race with which to primarily identify?

Bronwyn: No, other than when I'm answering forms—usually "other" or select "two or more races."

Me: What is a specific experience you recall (if any) where you felt like you had to "choose" a side when it came to your race or ethnicity? What was your feeling and response to this situation?

Bronwyn: When I participate in any activities where there is a high concentration of Asian people, I find myself leaning into my Asian roots and feeling a need to be a voice for them (us). Examples include: in school—orchestra, AP courses; and now, as an adult— Asian Diversity and Inclusion group at work.

Me: Based on your own experiences, what or who do you feel creates this type of pressure for multiracial individuals?

Bronwyn: Just the fact that labeling is a way society differentiates groups of people—and, unfortunately, I don't fit into any one of them. FORTUNATELY, this can also be a good thing because it makes people like us bridges to chasms created by divisions that come from binary labels. Labels are good to break down populations into more meaningful statistics, but when those labels create unhealthy divisions, we should stop to evaluate why we have them in the first place. Aren't we all placed on this Earth to figure out our own individual purpose and how to coexist with others'? To coexist, we need to understand each other, and it's way easier to do that when we can find ways to relate, starting with the things we have in COMMON, not where we differ.

Janet

Another individual I look up to, whom I met after attending a Charlotte CEO panel hosted by the YMCA, is Janet LaBar, president and CEO of the Charlotte Regional Business Alliance. When she was speaking about her experience childhood and getting to where she is now, Janet emphasized that, growing up as a Filipino girl, she was strongly encouraged to assimilate into American culture. She then talked about how her husband is a "White guy from New Jersey," and while she wanted to make sure her kids are assimilated, she did not want them to lose sight of their roots in her culture, which she was not as exposed to while young. She wanted to make sure her kids had that experience. While I did not get an opportunity to meet Janet that evening, I emailed her the morning after the panel, opening up about how I could relate to her story and would love to meet her. She emailed me back, and we set up a coffee meeting. We talked about all sorts of things, but I loved hearing about her desire for her kids to get the best of both worlds—assimilation and culture.

It was obvious upon my meeting Janet that she is a force to be reckoned with. Janet is a petite figure, but her presence in a room is massive and cannot be ignored. When she speaks, she is intelligent, thoughtful, and decisive. More importantly, she is an amazing listener. Since taking on her role at the Charlotte Regional Business Alliance, Janet has won several accolades recognizing her as one of the top leaders in Charlotte and the nation. Despite all her accolades, Janet continues to be one of the humblest human beings

I have ever met. While she is always excited to share the great things her team is doing, she doesn't ever take personal credit and is always looking for ways to leave the city of Charlotte better than she found it. I was very excited for Janet to share her perspective on this important topic of multiracial identity—specifically, as it relates to her children.

Me: What is your racial makeup?

Janet: I am Filipina, born in the United States. Both my parents are Filipino, from the Philippines, and my brothers and I are first-generation American.

Me: What is the racial makeup of your children?

Janet: My husband, James, and I have three beautiful children who are biracial—half Filipino and half White.

Me: Do people frequently ask you the question, "What are you?"

Janet: This was definitely more common growing up (in the South), though people have also asked me this as an adult. The more I experienced this question growing up, the more I learned to discern between genuine interest and inquisition laden with something more discriminate.

Me: Does this bother you (in the past or currently)?

Janet: There were times where I struggled between being proud to share my race and ethnicity and when I would put more emphasis on being American born. It all depended on who was asking and why I thought they were asking. It bothered me more as a young woman in my teens and twenties. Perhaps because, much of the time I received the question, it typically came from a man. And almost always, they wanted to assign a different race to me. Their guesses ranged from Mexican or Hawaiian to Native American or Indian. Rarely was their guess correct, and often, it left me feeling less valued as a complete person because they're inquiries did not go beyond my appearance.

Me: Have your children asked you about their own races? If so, how have you addressed their racial background with them?

Janet: James and I have always encouraged conversations with our children about race, the beauty of differences in people, and why we should value people for their differences both inside and out. When they were younger and first learning their words, we taught them they were Asian American. They were born in Phoenix, Arizona, which is home to a significant Latinx population, and then we moved to Portland, Oregon, where there were many other prevalent Asian communities. It was around that time when we shared more specifically that they are Filipino American. From children's books and involving them in preparing (and eating!) Filipino food, to attending Fil-Am festivals where they saw many other Filipinos and were exposed to folk dancing and arts and culture, we have celebrated with them the richness of our Philippine heritage.

Me: Do you think your children ever feel pressured to "choose" a certain race with which to primarily identify?

Janet: Our children are now middle- and elementary-school age. I don't see or hear of this pressure in our conversations with them. They self-identify as either Asian American, Filipino American, or half Filipino.

Me: Based on your own experiences and the experiences of your children, what or who do you feel creates this type of pressure for multiracial individuals?

Janet: Generally, I believe people are curious and well-intended. I also think diversity is embraced more today, and we are generally more accepting and perhaps more considerate in how we talk about race. My experience reveals another side of this, and I believe the pressure comes from some level of fear, insecurity, or [in]tolerance people might have about others who don't look like them. Unfortunately, I think we still default to what we see on the surface.

Me: What have you done, or what are you doing now, to make sure your children feel connected to the cultures that make up their background?

Janet: We continue to socialize the Filipino culture with our children through my side of the family. Several years ago, my parents gifted our oldest daughter a dictionary so she could look up words in Tagalog, the national language of the Philippines. My two older brothers and I were born in the late 1960s and '70s, respectively, and living in the South, I believe my parents—and many other Filipino families we knew—prioritized assimilation over bridging culture. They did not teach us Tagalog, and while I grew up hearing this and other Philippine dialects in the community of families my parents called friends, we are among a generation of Filipinos who do not speak the language. This makes it challenging to connect our children to race and culture simply because language is a gateway to deeper cognitive benefits. Having said this, we seek opportunities to instill in them the love of learning not only about the Filipino culture but others as well.

Chapter 8
The Roaring Twenties

In January 2020, a new virus originating out of Wuhan, China, called coronavirus, came to light in the American news media. It was not taken very seriously at first and was more or less presented as another form of SARS, which the United States had encountered about twelve years earlier, and SARS did not prove to have any long-lasting effects on the economy or American society at large.

The news media in America portrayed coronavirus, or COVID-19, as a virus from a faraway land that was being dealt with in other parts of the world that would never get near us. The prospect of the coronavirus having huge implications on our lives was minimal. Little did we know the American economy, jobs, travel, the education system, and everything dealing with life in America (and the rest of the world) would change dramatically within a matter of weeks.

When first hearing about it in the news, I just thought this would go through one or two news cycles, and then we would never hear about it again. Boy, was I wrong. The coronavirus very quickly reached the United States and immediately began wreaking havoc. States began putting in stay-at-home orders, some of which criminalized being out in public for any nonessential reasons. Americans lost jobs in the millions, causing the highest unemployment rate since the Great Depression. Those who still had jobs were working from home by mandate and constantly in fear of losing their livelihood. People were expected to wash or sanitize their hands everywhere they went. States shut down all nonessential businesses and mandated that people wear masks. People were dying. It was an absolute mess.

Many people blamed the Chinese for this virus. I had heard stories of people of East Asian descent getting attacked with racial slurs and, in some cases, physical violence at airports and other public places. Early on, some friends made jokes to me about how I already had the virus because I was part Asian. Being used to these types of jokes, I just laughed and brushed it off. It did make me sad to think that American citizens who "looked" Chinese or Asian in any type of way could be treated like this for something they had absolutely no control over. President Trump referred to the coronavirus as the "Chinese virus" and "Kung Flu," which the media had a field day in reporting initially ... until it became the norm. I never felt personally offended by any of these remarks, but when I started to hear Asian Americans speaking out, one of my first thoughts was, *Should I, too, be speaking out, even though I do not personally feel offended?* This was one of many moments where I was not quite sure which "side" to take, especially given the fact that we were now in a society where it seemed as though sides must be taken on every single topic.

On June 25, 2020, *TIME* published an article entitled, "'I Will Not Stand Silent.' 10 Asian Americans Reflect on Racism During the Pandemic and the Need for Equality," which discussed the discrimination being experienced by Asian Americans during the pandemic due to their race. "[A]nd now, as in the past, it's not just Chinese Americans receiving the hatred. Racist aggressors don't distinguish between different ethnic subgroups—anyone who is Asian or perceived to be Asian at all can be a victim."[56] The article goes through ten individuals who have experienced alarming incidents of racism based only on their appearances. While I could not relate to the stories from these individuals, I still felt a weird guilt because I felt I should be able to better empathize with the individuals discussed in this article.

As the world was in crisis mode during the coronavirus pandemic, the news was being watched and scrutinized more than ever. In late May 2020, a surveillance video out of Minneapolis went viral and shocked the world. The disturbing footage captured a Black man, George Floyd, getting pulled over, arrested, and placed in a chokehold by police officers for approximately four minutes and forty-five seconds. George Floyd died thereafter. This approximately nine-minute-long video breathed new life into a preexisting revolution in the midst of the pandemic: Black Lives Matter (BLM).

The BLM movement originally started in 2015 in response to multiple and repeated instances of what seemed to be excessive use of force from police when responding to a Black suspect, regardless of the severity of the alleged crime. The countermovement to the BLM movement was All Lives Matter, which made the point that Black lives weren't the only important ones, but so were all other races, including "blue" lives which were the police.

I believe the conversation surrounding race identity is especially important during this time in history given the revitalization of the Black Lives Matter movement in America and a push for *everyone*, not just Black individuals, to participate. Sometimes it's hard to figure out where we stand on social issues. But this one seemed an obvious concept we could all agree on: Black people should not be murdered because of the color of their skin. No one should be murdered because of the color of their skin nor on the sole basis of any other physical attribute.

When the BLM movement first started in 2015, it became a highly politicized issue. Fast-forward five years to 2020, as we approached another November election, and the issue became even more hotly politicized. This BLM movement, however, was different. It demanded those of other skin colors—especially Whites—to join in and speak out against police brutality against Black individuals on the basis of their skin color. The main purpose of this pressure put on *all* races was to emphasize that one doesn't have to be in a specific race or ethnicity to speak up for that group. Companies all around the globe enacted programs, campaigns, and initiatives to support the Black Lives Matter movement this time around.

As someone whose race was never quite clear to anyone else, I almost felt like an impostor speaking for either side in the past, but this movement empowered me not to be afraid to speak out against blatant racism. But being a mixed-race individual during this time was still confusing. It seemed like everyone in society and the media was hyper-focused on racial identity and the trials that came with being of color in America. The country's recognition of this is extremely important. Internally, I selfishly struggled with *Where do I fit in?*, though I was glad this BLM movement empowered all humans to join the fight for equality.

In a 2017 white paper from the *Journal of Education Controversy* entitled, "Practical Representation and the Multiracial Social Movement," the author acknowledged the pressing inquiries of: "[H]ow do Americans of different racial and cultural backgrounds who believe America should embrace multiracialism engage in action across racial lines to engender multi-racialist practices in the society at large? In doing so, how do different races of people get represented in the actual work of social and political change?"[57] The white paper—a government or authoritative report providing information on a particular issue[58]—goes on to address the fact that this type of pursuit would require a multiracial hegemonic project. It describes *hegemony* as "ideological consensus in civil society," and goes on to explain that, "[t]hough consensus may exist, it is always historically contingent and needs to be reproduced from generation to generation. This is especially true in liberal democracies where citizens exercise influence over political parties, electoral competition, and the shaping of the public policy agenda."[59]

This white paper addresses the question many mixed-race people have felt, and likely continue to feel, which is exacerbated when political movements that are occurring divide the country by race or some other cultural characteristic that leaves a multiracial individual feeling torn.

Amid all the protests going on along with the global pandemic, nature's destruction of the world in 2020 seemed to be unparalleled to any we had seen in the past—massive fires and winds on the West Coast, murder hornets, and many others. Then, almost exactly one year into the official pandemic, the world's attention shifted toward the controversy of "Asian Hate," a new antidiscrimination movement that essentially made its cameo in 2020. The topic had never previously made headlines in the way it did during that year.

Chapter 9

Stop Asian Hate and Black Lives Matter

The Stop Asian Hate movement was particularly interesting because it was something that, particularly at the beginning of the pandemic, became a heartbreaking problem, but not many people acknowledged the prejudice against Asian people prior to this. Because the first known coronavirus case was first reported in the city of Wuhan, China, this led to a significant increase in the amount of racism against Asians and Asian Americans.

The Center for the Study of Hate and Extremism at California State University, San Bernardino reported that, in the year 2020, hate crimes against Asians had increased by 150 percent.[60]

Since the beginning of the COVID-19 pandemic, according to the website stopaapihate.org created by an organization called Stop AAPI Hate, which is comprised of "communities [that] stand united against racism [...] hate against Asian American Pacific Islander communities has risen during the COVID-19 pandemic." Another article reported 3,795 hate crime incidents against Asian Americans from March 2020 through February 2021.[61]

Interestingly, a February 2021 study by the New York University College of Arts and Science found no actual increase of anti-Asian sentiment among the American population. However, it did suggest that individuals who were already prejudiced had felt somehow entitled by the pandemic to openly act on those prejudices.[62]

One of the most disturbing crime sprees against Asians that occurred during the pandemic was a series of mass shootings which occurred consecutively at three spas in the Atlanta area on March 16, 2021. Of the eight individuals killed, six were Asian women. The shooter was not charged with a hate crime, but many commentators characterized it as such. Per the police, the shooter said he did it because "he had a 'sexual addiction' and had carried out the shootings at the massage parlors to eliminate his 'temptation.'"[63]

To give examples of the media's treatment of hate crimes during this time, a BBC article listed headlines to demonstrate the type of violence occurring against Asian individuals during this time:

- An elderly Thai immigrant dies after being shoved to the ground.
- A Filipino American is slashed in the face with a box cutter.
- A Chinese woman is slapped and then set on fire.
- Eight people are killed in a shooting rampage across three Asian spas in one night.

These headlines do not even count those thousands of reported cases of being spat on and verbally harassed to incidents of physical assault. This demonstrates the notable surge in abuse since the start of the pandemic. Obviously, the victims of these crimes had absolutely nothing to do with the fact that a global pandemic was going on, but certain people filled with illogical prejudice used the pandemic as a pathetic excuse to misdirect their anger and frustration toward individuals whom they likely already had prejudicial feelings against but had never had a chance to express— until now. This was a bigot's big opportunity.[64]

The same BBC article noted that the FBI saw these hate crimes coming. "[T]he FBI warned at the start of the COVID-19 outbreak in the US that it expected a surge in hate crimes against those of

Asian descent. Federal hate crime data for 2020 showed there were a total of 279 anti-Asian incidents reported in 2020, which was a 77 percent increase since 2019."[65]

On May 20, 2021, with overwhelming support from Congress and sweeping support from both Democrats and Republicans,[66] President Biden signed into law the COVID-19 Hate Crimes Act to address the anti-Asian attacks that had been on the rise since the start of the pandemic. According to the bill, a US Justice Department official would be designated to expedite reviews of violence and hate crimes related to COVID-19. The bill also provides grants for state and local governments to improve their own reporting systems on similar crimes.[67]

The fact that we are still in a society where we have to utilize the law in order to prevent people from discriminating against certain racial groups is still truly shocking to me. While I recognize we are not in a "post-race" era, and it may take a significant number of years for us to get there (if ever), it is disheartening that in the United States of America—the known "melting pot" of the world—we are still having to pass laws to stop people from committing hate crimes against other humans for no reason other than the color of their skin. From the perspective of a multiracial individual, who never really cared or put the majority of my identity into my race, while I am grateful we live in a democratic society where these types of laws can be passed, I still find it hard to believe America had to resort to these types of measures in the year 2021.

As a multiracial individual, of course the happenings of Stop Asian Hate and BLM movements were infuriating; however, sometimes I was not sure exactly where I fit into the equation. In fact, I started writing this book in an app when I was unable to sleep, thinking about everything that was going on. I also began researching how others in my position felt about the historic race movement happening in our country.

In a June 2020 article entitled "My Message to Biracial People, Questioning Their Role in Black Lives Matter," the author states, "[a]s a biracial Black and White woman with white skin and brown, wavy hair, does my anger in response to the countless racist murders taking place across our country even matter? Because of how I look, I find myself questioning whether the pain I feel right now should even be acknowledged."[68]

This feeling of sitting on the sidelines of the Black Lives Matter and Stop Asian Hate movements was certainly relatable, as I felt compelled to speak up on these important issues. But also felt that my opinion was not nearly as important as those who were fully Black or Asian, and I would, in some way, be labeled as "privileged" for even having an opinion on this since I was part White. Looking back and thinking about my mindset from an objection perspective, it was ridiculous for me to think my opinion was less important just because I was of mixed race.

The author of the same article further notes that she continuously had to "reconcile[e] the duality of having privilege with responsibility" while also "recognize[ing] your own unique opportunities to create change when and where it is needed most." She stated that it is important for multiracial individuals to "[r]ecognize your own responsibility to end racism."[69]

In a July 2020 article entitled, "Black Lives Matter: Mixed-Race People Share Their Stories," Simone Stewart shared a five-minute video showing parents and young adults providing their perspectives on being mixed-race individuals during the 2020 BLM movement. Notably, the BLM movement had moved from the United States to the worldwide stage, as the individuals sharing their stories in this video in particular were from England. This goes to show that racial identity is not only limited to the United States and is faced by others throughout other parts of the world as well.

"[M]ixed-race people are the fastest-growing ethnic group, according to the last census. But what's it like growing up mixed-race in England, and what impact has the Black Lives Matter movement had?"[70]

Throughout the video, a parent and two young adults share their own personal stories. One part of the video shows a father with a multiracial child saying, "He's my son; he's my blood as well. You know, I don't look at a child as different to me."[71] The same father states later that his son will ask if they are going to a gathering of other children, "whether there will be any other mixed-race kids there," or whether there will be any other kids who look like him there. This is heartbreaking to the father, and when he brings it up to other parents, he typically receives a response of something like, "You're overthinking it." He then replies to them, "No, you're under-thinking it," demonstrating the importance of understanding the experience of multiracial children.[72]

Another young man speaks out by saying he did not even realize he was different until he started being bullied because of his mixed race.[73] The video shows a multiracial woman stating she experienced a great deal of racism growing up, having been called a "Black bastard" and a "Paki," which demonstrates the lack of education of individuals calling her that name. She further says her dad wanted to make sure she understood from a young age that the world would perceive her as Black—and he was right, as it became particularly apparent, in a majority White society, they were pointing out "Black" things about her rather than paying attention to the "White" things. She talks about how it is difficult for mixed-race people during the BLM movement because it sometimes comes off as "Black versus White" and can be confusing for mixed-race individuals, but of course, we all know it is about getting rid of racism as a whole that should be the focus.[74]

An article from the APA notes in response to the Stop Asian Hate movement:

> "[I]t's almost as if the public just discovered there's anti-Asian bias, discrimination, and hatred in this country," said Derald Wing Sue, PhD, a professor of psychology and education at Columbia University's Teachers College. "What's upsetting is it took so much violence for people to take the discrimination seriously. [...] [A]nother stereotype that contributes to ongoing anti-Asian bias and hate is the 'model minority' myth, the idea that Asian Americans are unilaterally successful and well adapted because

they are quiet, submissive, and hard-working. In fact, the stereotype was manufactured during the civil rights movement to weaponize Asian Americans against Black Americans, and it masks the diversity of the AAPI experience."[75]

The years 2020 and 2021 were really the first time in recent history where we had an intersection of significant movements for Blacks and Asians strongly advocating at the same time. The important thing to realize is neither of these were against each other; in fact, they were both on the same team for stopping racism.

An interviewee in the APA article noted, "It can also create the perception that Asian Americans are not considered to be people of color, and that we are immune to racism. [...] Therefore, when people do speak up about it, our experiences are actually dismissed."[76]

The same can be said for mixed-race individuals. Where do we fit in, particularly in a world where so many people want to place individuals in one "box"? There is no right answer to this question other than to do our best to take race completely out of the equation when creating perceptions of ourselves in our own minds and perceptions of others.

A publication from *Pew Research Center* entitled "Race in America 2019," dated April 9, 2019, discusses a study that reveals:

Blacks are also far more likely than other groups to say their race is very or extremely important to how they think about themselves, but half or more Hispanics and Asians also say their racial or ethnic background is central to their overall identity; only 15 percent of Whites say the same. About three-quarters of Black adults (74 percent) say being Black is very important to how they think about themselves, including 52 percent who say it is extremely important. About six-in-ten Hispanics (59 percent) say being Hispanic is extremely or very important to their identity, and 56 percent of Asians say the same about being Asian. In contrast, only 15 percent of Whites say being

White is as important to their identity; 19 percent of Whites say it is moderately important, while 18 percent say it's only a little important, and about half (47 percent) say their race is not at all important to how they think about themselves. Among Blacks and Whites, those younger than thirty see their race as less central to their identity than their older counterparts. Still, majorities of Blacks—and relatively small shares of Whites across age groups—say their race is extremely or very important to how they think about themselves. Hispanics born in another country (65 percent) are more likely than those born in the US (52 percent) to say being Hispanic is at least very important to their overall identity.[77]

While I found it surprising how individuals with one specific race overwhelmingly made race an important part of their identity versus other races, this study shows part of the reason as to why the racial divide during the 2020 BLM movement appeared to be more "Black versus White" instead of there being a focus on trying to rid the world of racism as a whole. This is also understandable because the BLM movement was initially motivated specifically by deaths of Black individuals by White police officers; however, it certainly made the BLM movement confusing for me as a mixed-race individual during this time, as I felt conflicted about speaking out about the issue. It was almost as if I had an underlying guilt for being half White during this time.

In a *Vox* article entitled, "The Loneliness of Being Mixed Race in America," from January 2021, the author interviewed six multiracial individuals about how they were feeling during the 2020 BLM movement. One person discussed his own struggle with being of mixed race: "I had to figure out the language to describe myself." Another said, "I've found terms to identify myself that feel somewhat comfortable but also somewhat unsatisfying."[78] While each individual interviewed for the article had different experiences and perspectives, each story had the same general theme: it was, and still is, difficult to describe themselves, particularly during a time in the world's history where there is so much division regarding race.[79]

Chapter 10

What Now?

According to "Summary of Stages of Racial Identity Development," the way to resolve biracial identity tensions, which can also be applied to multiracial and racially ambiguous identity tensions, is to take any of the following steps that work best for the individual seeking to relieve internal identity tensions:

1. Accept the identity society assigns—identify with the group into which others assume the biracial individual most belongs, usually with family support.
2. Identify with both (or all) heritage groups, depending on social and personal support.
3. Choose one group, independent of social pressure, to identify yourself in a particular way.
4. Identify as a new racial group—move fluidly among racial groups but identify most strongly with other biracial people, regardless of specific heritage backgrounds.[80]

Actionable Steps for Multiracial Individuals

I have thought of the following additional actionable steps on how to overcome identity crisis from being racially ambiguous.

1. Embrace your culture to the extent that you feel comfortable. If you, like me, sometimes feel as though you are an impostor in your own skin, you have absolutely no reason to feel that way. Instead, find ways to learn about the cultures that make up your being. Ask questions of your family members about ancestors so you can relate to them, even if they are no longer living. Learn to cook food from one of your home countries. I am not a gourmet chef by any means, but I found that one way to try and connect myself and my loved ones to a different culture than the one I am made up of is food.

My brother sent me a Filipino cookbook in 2022, which is one of my favorite gifts I've received to date. Some recipes I have tried are the chicken *sotanghon* soup (which is chicken soup with glass noodles and pork-scallion meatballs) and Filipino spaghetti hotdogs (which is exactly what it sounds like!). While I am still a novice at cooking in general, and certainly brand new at cooking Filipino food, giving it a try provides me with a whole new perspective on connecting with the culture. Even just cooking Filipino food and enjoying it with the ones I love make me feel all the more connected to my Filipino heritage.

Ask for family recipes. If you can't find any from family members, look up recipes online or, like my brother did for me, get a cookbook specific to your culture with dishes that originated from your heritage. You have a great and unique opportunity to have diverse tastes and histories. Don't be afraid to ask questions. It's never too late to participate in the various cultures that make you who you are.

2. Don't identify yourself based only on your race.

The ways in which race identity seems to define people in today's society are countless, but you should not have to let that completely take over your identity as a whole. You are a unique individual, and that is what makes you amazing. Taking pride in one's identity is wonderful, particularly for racial groups who were historically conditioned to be "ashamed" of their race—which is essentially every race that is not traditionally White. Non-White people wanting to celebrate their identity and culture as a major part of who they are is not something that should be rejected. However, there is more to a person than only racial identity. Taking into consideration that it is wonderful to have your race as part of your identity, you can also define your personhood by your interests, passions, treatment toward others, skills, achievements, travel, friends, and family, by bringing joy and adding value to the lives of others. Be the author and star of the life you live. Create your own life.

3. Don't let anyone make you feel inadequate because you are mixed race.

In the *Vox* article discussed in Chapter 9, the author points out, "[a]s the mixed population grows in size, it will likely continue to serve as projections for people to sort through America's complex race relations. But what about the experiences of those who are actually multiracial? Studies illustrate a group of people who struggle with questions of identity and where to fit in, often feeling external pressures to 'choose' a side. There's evidence that mixed-race people have higher rates of mental health issues and substance abuse too."[81]

The article further states:

Americans, for the most part, don't think having a racial background that includes more than one race has been an advantage or a disadvantage in their life. But to the extent that it has mattered, more say their racial background has been beneficial than say it has been detrimental. This is particularly the case among biracial adults who are White and Asian. [...] A majority (60 percent) of multiracial adults say they have, at times, felt pride in their mixed racial background, a sentiment shared by about a half or more across multiracial groups. Three-quarters of those who are White and Asian say they are proud of having a racial background that includes more than one race, as do 64 percent of White and Black, 57 percent of White and American Indian, and 54 percent of Black and American Indian biracial adults; about half (53 percent) of multiracial adults who are White, Black, and American Indian also say they have felt this way.[82]

I agree I do not feel that having a multiracial background has been detrimental to me, but I have not seen it as an advantage or a disadvantage. I have only recently learned to have real pride in having a multiracial background because it creates a certain type of uniqueness in society that should be embraced and celebrated. This is not the time to be ashamed; this is the time to be proud that you share multiple racial identities and do not need to be defined by any one of them.

4. Support groups discussing multiracial identity.
There are groups within communities that exist to provide a community for multiracial people—and those who want to better understand multiracial people—to express themselves, connect, share, and discuss complex issues and ideas. If there is not one in your community, and there is enough of a population of multiracial individuals, why not consider

starting one? This could help you and others open up and discuss similar experiences and how they are dealing with similar issues.

5. Understand that there are different frameworks recognized for acceptance of one's race.
Become familiar with them to assist with explaining how you feel at any given point in your life. There are various frameworks for stages of identity development. While I am not a psychologist, it was helpful to understand the different frameworks so I could better explain why I felt the way I did during certain times of my life. Specifically, what was most helpful in understanding myself was the continuum of racial identity framework because I believe I started out blending my mixed-race identity, with emphasis on the White race. However, eventually, the blending shifted, and I now identify as more of an equal blend of White and Filipino. This continuum framework helped me understand I do not necessarily have to identify with one race or both races at all times but can shift throughout my existence. These frameworks are useful tools for self-reflection and building empathy and understanding of people who are situated differently from you. It is also important to note that people might visit and revisit different stages during different points in their lives. The frameworks are as follows:

Biracial (Poston)
1. Personal Identity: sense of self unrelated to ethnic grouping; occurs during childhood
2. Choice of Group: as a result of multiple factors, individuals feel pressured to choose one racial or ethnic group identity over another (BLM too)
3. Categorization: choices influenced by status of group, parental influence, cultural knowledge, appearance

4. Enmeshment/Denial: guilt and confusion about
   choosing an identity that isn't fully expressive of
   all their cultural influences; denial of differences
   between the racial groupings; possible exploration
   of the identities not chosen in stages two and three
5. Appreciation: of multiple identities
6. Integration: sense of wholeness, integrating
   multiple identities

Continuum of Biracial Identity Model (Kerry Ann Rockquemore and Tracey Laszloffy)

1. Does not seek to categorize individuals into a single
   identity; acknowledges continuum
2. Some people may choose to identify singularly with
   one of their identities
3. Some may blend with primary emphasis on one
   identity and a secondary emphasis on the other
4. Some may blend two (or more) identities with
   equal emphasis

Resolutions of Biracial Identity Tensions (Maria P. P. Root)

1. Accept the identity society assigns: identify with
   the group into which others assume the biracial
   individual most belongs, usually with family support
2. Identify with both (or all) heritage groups, depending
   on social and personal support
3. Choose one group, independent of social pressure, to
   identify yourself in a particular way
4. Identify as a new racial group: move fluidly among
   racial groups but identify most strongly with other
   biracial people, regardless of specific
   heritage backgrounds

Integrated Model (John and Joy Hoffman)

1. Conformity: first stage, people of color and Whites feel they are just "regular Americans." Unconsciously, members of both groups strive to emulate Whiteness in actions, speech, dress, beliefs, and attitudes because Whiteness is perceived as positive.
2. People of color—dissonance: discovery that race or gender may preclude them from benefits Whites or males receive. They start to feel confused about beliefs they held about America and themselves as they begin to see how racism and sexism may be impacting them.
3. Immersion: questions and disillusionment can lead to the immersion stage where they feel angry; what might people of color do with this anger?
4. Emersion: anger about racism is directed toward Whites; leads people to feel they can only belong with others in their own racial group who understands them.
5. Internalization: occurs when people realize there are negative qualities among all races, and White people are not the enemy and some thing needed to be fought against; also people manifest desire to have control over who they want to be—more than just a race or gender.
6. Integrative awareness—both Whites and people of color: Whites and people of color both come to conclusions that there is much more to them than their race or gender. Both groups are able to positively identify with their own racial group while also acknowledging that other aspects of their identity (gender, talents, and abilities, unique experiences) contribute to their personhood.[83]

My hope is we can all make it to integrative awareness—where no one is judging or making assumptions of others based solely on race, gender, or any other immutable characteristic, but we recognize it is part of who someone is as a whole person. I also want multiracial individuals to recognize they do not need to be defined by any specific race, color, or any other outward-facing attribute; they are much more than the "box" they check on a college application or census.

6. Overcome Impostor Syndrome.
In an August 2020 article published in *Mental Health America*, Jennifer Cheang points out that multiracial people experience impostor syndrome differently than monoracial individuals.

> [Multiracial people] face unique stressors and often find it is difficult to connect with others—even with other multiracial people. More often than not, the parents of multiracial people will not necessarily understand their struggles. Even among multiracial people, their experiences are so unique, talking with other multiracial people can feel disjointed, and there can be a failure to connect. [...] When you don't feel like you "belong" to a group of people, it can make you question your experiences and sense of identity, especially when how identify is often rooted in the way the world sees you. [...] Remember: you are not a racial imposter. You get to define how you identify. You are enough, and you do not need to justify your existence to anyone.[84]

This is your reminder that you are not alone, and you are not an impostor just because you look different from your family, friends, and those you see in the media.

7. Journal.

Simply the act of writing this has made me feel like a whole new person. Journaling your thoughts and feelings about a particular situation, or even just generally, has proven to be therapeutic for many reasons. Putting something down on paper to vent, analyze, and document is a feeling unlike any other. This will help you gather your thoughts, organize them in a physical form, and analyze why you are feeling the way you do. You don't necessarily have to journal every day, but it could be a useful tool in dealing with a topic that goes largely unnoticed and is not talked about very often.

For me, I felt the urge to write this book after different experiences dealing with racial identity, many of which you have read about in this book. There are surely more experiences I have not shared because I do not recall them. If I had written them down at the time, along with expressions of my feelings, I believe it would have forced me to write this book sooner and provided me with more therapy, as well as more people with the ability to relate and understand sooner.

8. Community.

Outside a support-group type of community, community involvement in more diverse groups that do not look like you is a great way of understanding and appreciating different cultures. Examples of this are: volunteering with people in a more diverse part of town than the part of town in which you live, organizing or participating in community events that highlight other cultures, joining groups within your profession or organization that are intentionally multicultural, and participating in open mic and spoken word events that highlight identity, social justice, and intersectionality. In fact, my brother recently invited me—through a lawyer he knows in Seattle—to a group of Filipino lawyers who connect throughout the country. I was so thankful my brother brought this up to me and am thrilled to become involved in this community, along with the other lawyer communities in which I already participate.

9. Travel.

American author Mark Twain once wrote in his book *The Innocents Abroad* that "[t]ravel is fatal to prejudice, bigotry, and narrow-mindedness, and many of our people need it sorely on these accounts. Broad, wholesome, charitable views of men and things cannot be acquired by vegetating in one little corner of the earth all one's lifetime."[85]

American historian, author, and women's suffrage activist Miriam Beard once said, "Certainly, travel is more than the seeing of sights; it is a change that goes on, deep and permanent, in the ideas of living."[86]

These thoughts on travel ring especially true on the topic of racial ambiguity and the issue of feeling out of place or being an impostor in any setting in which you may find yourself. While growing up, my family did not travel much—especially compared to other families in my school—but each time we did, I came back with a more open perspective than I had before. For example, when I was a sophomore in high school, I traveled with my parents to Zurich, Switzerland, and the Swiss Alps. This was the first time I had been to Europe and one of my first times skiing. Neither of my parents ski, so I went up the mountain by myself while they waited for me in the lodge. While skiing, I got lost and could not read the signs because they were in German. When I tried to ask people where I should go, I experienced similar language barriers. Ultimately, a Dutch man saw I was confused, helped me find the easiest way down the mountain, and even coached me on the best way to ski. After this experience and upon returning to Charlotte, I became so much more appreciative of other cultures and people generally, remembering we are all humans just trying to do our best. While this was not necessarily a "cultural" experience I learned to appreciate, the fact that I was lost and in need of help in a foreign land—and someone who spoke an entirely different language than me was able to recognize that and give me the help I needed—made me realize we are all connected and much more alike than we are different in this world.

Travel is also a privilege restricted to individuals of a certain class and higher, and many people today cannot afford to travel. In fact, I did not start traveling more until during and after law school when I traveled to different cities for law school-sponsored events and after law school when I purposefully saved up to travel more. My brother developed and directed the Philippines Study Abroad Program as a professor at the University of Washington, which is an example of a way individuals can travel through educational programs. If you have the opportunity and means to do so, travel allows people to experience entirely different worlds, cultures, and perspectives that are not otherwise available in the town in which they grew up. Getting out of one's comfort zone to travel and experience new places and meet different types of people can greatly assist with feelings of being an outsider. At the end of the day, we are all human and have different gifts to offer the world. Travel reinforces this belief and is truly the ultimate connector of us all.

10. Determine what makes you you.

Understand your values. Recognizing it is more important to understand someone's values, experiences, and passions—instead of focusing primarily on someone's racial background—should help you understand the need to determine what *your* values are. I used to struggle with what exactly my "values" were, but I took some time to educate myself and read articles on values, which helped me realize I was not the only one who had trouble defining them. Apparently, defining values is a common issue among individuals who are struggling with finding their own identity. Many of the articles I found discussed core values, defined what they are, and provided a list of core values I could use to define what mine are. Each article had a different variety of core values on their respective lists. The words on these lists that stood out to me the most were things you could not imagine yourself without—those are your "values."

Reading these lists was helpful because it allowed me to recognize that my top three core values are: adaptability, perseverance, and positivity. Of course, values such as faith, family, and friends on many of the lists are a given; however, I cannot imagine existing in this world without having the values of adaptability, perseverance, and positivity. Adaptability and perseverance go hand in hand, as both of these require fortitude to move forward despite change or difficulties. Without positivity, it can be hard to adapt and persevere through changing and difficult times. Positivity has always been a top value of mine, but I did not realize the benefits of being an optimist in getting through challenging circumstances until I had to face trying situations, such as being hit by a car when I was ten years old or my law school being shut down a couple of short years after I graduated. Prior to fully understanding my values, my worth depended on how others perceived me, such as my level of outward achievement, but that has since changed because I am much more concerned with my own personal values and whether I am living them out every day. My goal in asking you what your values are is for you to realize them yourself and think about how you can live those out every day in the most fulfilling way possible.

One of my mentors, Sara Holtz, has a podcast called *Advice to My Younger Me*[87] and is the author of a book entitled the same,[88] and in one episode, she discusses with a guest of hers that the best way to find out your strengths at work is to ask those whom you work closely with. While this concept seems obvious because those we work most closely with undoubtedly know what we do best, it was groundbreaking for me to hear because I have never previously had the confidence to ask that type of question. The same applies not only to work but in life generally. Ask those around you: What is the "essence" of you? In other words, what aspects of you make you unique? This is important because it helps to further realize your value as a unique individual in the world, apart from your external appearance or others' perception of what your external appearance might (or might not) mean.

11. Generally, be more open to people of different races and cultures and educate others to do the same.
A Pew Research survey found that "multiracial adults may have a more open and understanding approach to people of other races and cultures. About six-in-ten (59 percent) multiracial Americans believe their mixed racial background has made them more open to cultures other than their own, and about as many (55 percent) have felt they are more understanding of people of different racial backgrounds.[89]

12. Help your children feel comfortable in their own skin.
As a mixed-race individual, if or when you have children, they will undoubtedly also be of mixed race. It is important to pass along the confidence and assurance you have taken from this book and ensure your children are comfortable in their own skin. A November 2019 article from *Psychology Today* entitled, "Growing Up Multiracial" discusses why raising children to be comfortable in their own skin is important.

Perhaps not surprisingly, multiracial children may encounter some identity development experiences children with one racial background do not undergo. Parents and adults responsible for the emotional and psychological well-being of multiracial children may be facing issues they never came across themselves ... [p]arents and caregivers can positively influence multiracial children's self-concept and happiness by communicating acceptance of children's self-exploration and self-descriptions. Racial identity is not static and typically changes over time and across situations ... [a]dults can communicate a positive and open environment about multiracial identity to their children by introducing and emphasizing: 1) Multiracial-affirmative stories, coloring books, and toys; 2) open-ended avenues for expression, such as creative writing, painting, and drawing; 3) positive aspects and strengths of being multiracial; 4) dialogue about race and listening supportively to any hurtful racial comments their children may have experienced; and 5) multiracial role models and peers.[90]

These are actionable steps parents of multiracial children can take in order to ensure their children grow up as comfortable as possible in their own beautiful skin.

13. Know you are the future of humanity.
There is nothing to be ashamed of for being comprised of different races and being racially ambiguous. In fact, racially ambiguous people are often thought of as the future of America and humanity. This is primarily because racially ambiguous individuals represent what all people will look like at some point in the future, as predicted by the 2013 National Geographic article that printed a photo of a mixed-race individual to show what the "average American" will look like in 2050, along with the articles cited in this book that indicate multiracial individuals are becoming

progressively more common in America.[91] When individuals from all over the globe pair up, monoracial will no longer be the norm.

14. Get to know the Bill of Rights for People of Mixed Heritage.
A December 2018 article entitled, "Bill of Rights for Mixed Heritage" discusses a "Bill of Rights" written by Maria P. Root. "In the United States, people who seem ethnically ambiguous have remained either invisible or forced to pick a 'side' based on the way they look. Although this was published so many years ago, it is still relevant and important for people to read, acknowledge, and share widely."[92]

Below is the text of the Bill of Rights for People of Mixed Heritage we should share with those who are, and even those who are not, in the same boat:

I HAVE THE RIGHT ...
- Not to justify my existence in this world.
- Not to keep the races separate within me.
- Not to justify my ethnic legitimacy.
- Not to be responsible for people's discomfort with my physical or ethnic ambiguity.

I HAVE THE RIGHT ...
- To identify myself differently than strangers expect me to identify.
- To identify myself differently than how my parents identify me.
- To identify myself differently than my brothers and sisters.
- To identify myself differently in different situations.

I HAVE THE RIGHT …
- To create a vocabulary to communicate about being multiracial or multiethnic.
- To change my identity over my lifetime—and more than once.
- To have loyalties and identification with more than one group of people.
- To freely choose whom I befriend and love.[93]

Actionable Steps for Society At Large

Again, I am not a psychologist, nor am I a politician; however, I have also thought of actionable steps for what may help society in recognizing the importance of multiracial identities:

1. Education.

Education—as early on as possible—is crucial to understanding perspectives of multiracial and racially ambiguous individuals. For example, as previously discussed, the Seattle Public School system now offers Filipino American history curriculum to satisfy the district's US history requirement for high school students. While it is not necessary for all high school students throughout the United States to learn about Filipino American history, this type of education for *any* culture can help to normalize multicultural individuals within American society.

2. Greater recognition of mixed-race individuals in pop culture and acknowledgement of such.

We are no longer in a world where people can be defined by one or two syllables. We are increasingly more unique and more complex humans. This is the beauty of America, and it should be shared and acknowledged. Additionally, whether you are multiracial or not, you have most likely encountered someone who is racially ambiguous, and you may have presumed that individual to be monoracial, multiracial, or not thought about it at all. With all this information available to you now, you can begin to understand more deeply the experiences of racially ambiguous individuals. As the *Very Well* article stated, "[r]acial ambiguity is becoming progressively more common and is an important experience to understand."[94]

3. Race as a nonpartisan issue.

Unfortunately, the issue of racial relations tends to come off as an issue that is more "liberal" because it is not a traditional conservative value that is talked about comfortably in a room full of old, White men. It is a social issue, which is typically seen as falling squarely in the "liberal" column. Stop the madness. The Black Lives Matter movement is still seen as a liberal issue, which is sad. Instead, the idea of racial relations is a social issue that affects everyone—and will continue to affect everyone going forward—so it should be embraced by both conservatives and liberals alike. British sociologist Stuart Hall proposed that, in order to allow for real change in the race conversation, "efforts to build a multiracial hegemony must be waged primarily at the local level where there is the potential for face-to-face engagement and greater honesty than at the abstract level of national politics."[95]

4. Using racial ambiguity as a way to educate others.

I believe having a multiracial background has generally made me open to other cultures and more understanding of different racial backgrounds; however, I have never seen myself as an ambassador who can bring people of different races together. I am not alone in this.

According to a Pew Research study, "just 19 percent [of multiracial individuals] say they have ever felt like a go-between, or 'bridge,' between different racial groups, while 80 percent have not felt this way."[96] This shows there is power in being multiracial in the sense that you have the unique ability to bring different races together merely by your understanding of living your life in a state of ambiguity between more than one race.

5. Training on bias and stereotypes (unconscious or otherwise).

In school, the workplace, even social organizations, like any other type of bias training, the first issue that needs to be addressed is admitting we, as humans, stereotype each other constantly—whether consciously or subconsciously—and recognizing when we do it. We, as a society, tend to be lazy and use stereotypes to create efficiencies to put certain people in "boxes," allowing us to more quickly process what type of person they are, or in which behaviors they are most likely to engage. Of course, this is usually far from the truth, as we are all human beings who are much more complex and unique than predictable behavior stereotypes promote. If people can recognize we have these stereotypes, then we will be more likely to suppress those human responses when encountered. Stereotypes come in many forms. The type I discuss here is the need to assign one race to another individual in order to allow the brain to process how that individual may act in a certain situation. Those whose race is ambiguous, particularly those who are of mixed race, present a challenge for those who require stereotypes and "box-checking." That said, if we can add some type of bias training, not only for those of other races but also include those whose race is ambiguous, it would benefit all people in resisting the urge to engage in this human behavior.

Understand that certain definitions used in racial conversations are viewed differently from a multiracial or racially ambiguous individual's perspective, which are the following:

Colorism.

Within communities of color, there are examples of how lighter-skinned or people who have more traditionally European features are favored as better or more desirable in these communities. It is important to recognize how even within our communities, we uphold ideals of White supremacy based on one's "proximity to Whiteness." Multiracial individuals who are darker-skinned, compared to the lighter-skinned "ideal of beauty" held by their communities, can be mocked, shunned, and discriminated against by people within their own community.

Exclusion and isolation.
Multiracial individuals can often feel excluded from their communities. You're "too much" of something or "not enough." My own extended family was very loving and accepting of my little, mixed family, but there was always an internal sense of being different. I didn't look like them, couldn't speak like them, and didn't have the same experiences as them.

Privilege.
It is important to recognize for some multiracial individuals that you have a lot of privilege, depending on the way people see you. For example, lighter-skinned, White-adjacent, or White-passing multiracial people have significantly different experiences than others. While this privilege doesn't negate negative experiences due to identity or other struggles of being multiracial, it's important to realize the privilege that comes with being able to "come out" as an identity, which is different than for people who are automatically stereotyped based on their appearance. Even if you aren't accepted by your community—especially if you have Black or Indigenous heritage—it's still important to show up for issues of injustice anyway and use the privilege you do hold to navigate spaces others cannot. This is a tough pill to swallow. I have been there. But it is something we need to understand, learn, and grow from.[97]

These definitions come from the article written by a woman who is multiracial—specifically, Puerto Rican and Chinese. I can relate to her commentary on the definitions of each of these. Like her, I am lucky my extended family on both sides—the fully Filipino side and the fully White side—did not exclude or isolate me because I did not completely look like one or the other. They accepted me based on who I was as a person rather than focused on whether they felt I was "enough" of one race or the other. Additionally, like the author of the same article, I recognize the privilege that comes with being multiracial and understand I should use this privilege to be a bridge between races, with the objective to strengthen the voice of those who may not hold a similar type of privilege.

6. Dear media, just be better, please.
In recent years, Hollywood has—at least externally—pursued further transparency regarding diversity and has celebrated inclusivity. Per the CARD report, "continued evaluation, increased advocacy, and greater transparency are necessary to transform an industry that has profited from invisibility into one that can celebrate inclusivity."[98] Similar to the Stuart Hall findings,[99] it is just as important for Hollywood to acknowledge the lack of diversity—not only in representation, but also in production of film and television—properly represent real people in the world.

7. Never stop learning.
Something I did not receive in my years of great education was learning more about multiracial identities. The article from *Best Colleges* proposes that this type of education remains critical to supporting all college and university students. The article provides a list of resources to help strengthen understanding:

> 1) The Multiracial Network, organized within the Coalition for Multicultural Affairs, supports the creation of inclusive spaces within postsecondary education for people who identify as multiracial, multiethnic, and transracial, and those with fluid

racial identities; 2) The American Psychological Association provides an overview of various studies about biracial identities, including personal narratives; 3) Created by Steven F. Riley, MixedRaceStudies.org offers a comprehensive look into issues regarding multiracialism. Topics include historical, psychological, and personal resources; 4) The *Multiracial Activist*, an online publication, dedicates its journalistic coverage to biracial and multiracial people, transracial adoptees, and interracial couples and families; 5) Surveys by the Pew Research Center, which provide a voice to individuals with multiracial heritages; and 6) Other: *Mixed Race in America*, a podcast created by the *Washington Post* in 2017, explores the identities of multiracial people through a five-part storytelling series.[100]

As for the Pew surveys, many of those were cited in this book and provide a helpful tool for those who are of mixed-race heritage in understanding that others are just like you, and for those who are not of mixed-race heritage to foster understanding of what multiracial individuals experience and their perspective overall.

In addition, the Family Institute at Northwestern University suggested:

> To adapt to this changing landscape, it is important to be knowledgeable about the history of race, as well as current trends and factors influencing the racial identity development of multiracial individuals. Research clearly shows that individuals who are raised in supportive families, neighborhoods, and social networks, and who attend schools with diverse populations, tend to develop a healthy self-confidence and racial identity. Caregivers, both directly and indirectly, play an essential role in shaping the racial identity of their children. Caregivers often oversee choices regarding which community to live in, the schools their children attend, and provide (or limit) opportunities to discuss and explore

racial or ethnic heritage. Families are encouraged to increase their own awareness, knowledge, and skills, and to support open communication about racial or ethnic heritage. Resources are to help families support multiracial youth in their unique identity development. If problems develop, caregivers might consider counseling for their children to support positive racial identity development, as well as to help them cope with distress in a supportive environment.[101]

I feel fortunate I was born in a city with a diverse population (Seattle), even though the neighborhood and schools I grew up in did not have as much diversity relative to the city itself. I was exposed to individuals from other schools who had more diverse populations, along with my brother's group of friends who were similarly much more diverse. When I moved to the South, it was a culture shock, not because I was not accustomed to being surrounded by White peers (because I was used to being surrounded by White peers in my school and in my neighborhood growing up) but because the idea of someone looking like me—different and racially ambiguous—was foreign to the majority of the peers I had in Charlotte due to the demographic of the city itself. While I am grateful for the education I received and the fact that I generally had a happy childhood growing up, looking back, having an understanding of my unique identity and educating myself on ways in which to cope with potential identity tensions would have been beneficial in the environment in which I grew up.

8. **Viewing "diversity" the way a mature multiracial person would view it—as one part of our identity but not all-encompassing.**
A July 2018 article on the evolution of mixed-race identity in the twenty-first century discusses the Hapa Project, in which photographer Kip Fulbeck took more than a thousand photos of mixed-race individuals.[102]

The photos are labeled with the various racial and ethnic groups each person identifies as belonging to. It brings to mind census or job application categories, but while everyone in this series might simply be put in "Asian" or "Native Hawaiian or Other Pacific Islander" on such forms, here they get to attest to a wide range of backgrounds. Pushing against the basic nature of ideas around identity reveals the limitations in our thought and institutions and hopefully awakens us to an expanded understanding of the subject, not just as it pertains to race but to a mosaic of other qualities—gender, sexuality, class, ideology, spirituality, and much more.

In just fifteen years, the explosion of the internet has allowed for more involved, varied, and purposeful construction of one's identity than at any previous point in human history. With this has come greater interrogation of just what identity is and what it means, both on a cultural and personal level. The constant debates around the definitions and utility of identity politics are one obvious example, as is the discourse around minority representation in art and media.[103]

Exposing people to innovative exhibits such as the Hapa Project will allow others to see a glimpse of mixed-race individuals from a different perspective and hopefully leave perceiving them in a different light.

9. Utilize perspectives of multiracial individuals.

What if the rest of the world looked at others in the same way certain racially ambiguous or multiracial individuals view others? As psychology studies state, multiracial children do not start out with any type of identity in their specific race(s) and, instead, just want to get to know individuals by understanding what makes them unique. Moreover, according to the APA article previously discussed, "[c]ompared to monoracial people, multiracial people are *less susceptible to race-based memory biases*."[104] This means multiracial individuals do not put as much weight on someone's race or perceived race as monoracial individuals typically do.

The need for conformity society has created has completely blundered all hope for individuals recognizing and appreciating their unique contributions to the world—not only based on the way they look on the outside but also what is on the inside: brain, heart, background, experiences, ideas, hopes, and dreams. If society worries less about individuals' immutable characteristics, such as race, we would be better positioned to acknowledge and celebrate what we are bringing to the world that is different, unique, and truly worth knowing in a person.

The APA article goes on to note:

> For multiracial people, race represents a less visible aspect of identity (like other less visible traits, such as personality traits) that has the potential to provoke unpredictable reactions from perceivers. [...] For monoracial people, in contrast, race is highly visible. Perceivers rarely make mistakes when judging races of monoracial targets, indicating that monoracial people should be able to predict, with a high degree of accuracy, how others will see them. As a result, race should not represent a characteristic of the self monoracial people need others to verify. Instead, monoracial people likely view their own race as immutable and incontrovertible—as a "fact" about the self.[105]

While I am not proposing race should be prohibited as being a part of an individual's identity, I believe it does not have to be the one trait people focus on—the end all be all. Society's obsession with race as far as identity is the reason we are still having discord in racial relations.

After a mixed individual goes through an inevitable, initial identity crisis (typically more than one), accepts that the person they are does not need to fall into one "box," and recognizes the value of being a complex and unique individual, that individual's outlook on the world completely shifts. For me, once I finally understood my value as a one-of-a-kind individual, I became more empathetic and stopped judging others around me for circumstances I may not understand. For example, if someone cuts me off in traffic or aggressively walks in front of me in the line for coffee, I used to automatically think that person must be a terrible, rude person, who intentionally did something to harm me. In reality, it is more likely this incident had nothing to do with me, and the person who cut me off in traffic or walked in front of me in the coffee line was experiencing something difficult, going through a hard time, or simply trying to get through the day.

As humans, we typically assume the worst about other people. Everyone has heard the example of the person who walks into a meeting late, and everyone else in the room automatically assumes negative traits about the person—even if it was the first time that person had ever been late in their entire life. Jumping to conclusions about other people is a large part of the reason stereotyping exists, not just in race but also in other social situations. Instead, if we decide to treat others with grace and assume the best about others, rather than automatically assume the worst, we can all experience much more harmony in this thing called life. Each person brings a unique perspective to the world that is inherently valuable because without each individual's own thoughts and perspectives, the world would be a much more boring place.

It is not necessary for us to be "color-blind"—as humans, being truly "color-blind" simply is not possible—but instead recognize the inherent value each individual brings as a complex and multifaceted human being, worth more than perceived race or any other external characteristic. Moreover, the concept of "color-blindness" is inherently a privileged one because someone claiming they "don't see race" is erasing an entire aspect of a person's identity and potentially cultural heritage. This is typically associated with the privilege of Whiteness, as White is the societal "default," and White people rarely, if ever, have to think about race in the way non-White people do. Those of mixed race are just as conscious about their race and how they are perceived as any other human;

this allows them to be more empathetic to, and understanding of, those of *all* races, including other multiracial individuals.

As a multiracial individual matured in learning about identity and how racial identity plays a factor in self-identity, I tend to see race more as something similar to a shoe size, a physical characteristic that does not define who I am, nor who anyone else is. Shoe size should not be something that defines who you are or what you do (unless your job is to be the man with comically large feet at the circus or county fair).

Multiracial individuals are more likely to recognize earlier in life that a person should not be judged based on what you see, but instead that each person is a mixture of complex traits with unique thoughts and individuality only that person can share with the world. We are all "mixed" kids at heart, trying to figure out where we fit in, wondering who will accept us for the whole, unique individual we are, and overall seeking to be understood.

Teaching others that perception of an individual's external characteristics is human nature but also stereotypical by nature. Judging individuals only by external characteristics is part of the reason racism exists. In order to achieve the type of diversity and inclusion that has been fought for by thought leaders throughout the past few decades, we must recognize we cannot stop humans from engaging in behavior that is true to human nature but instead find a way to recognize our own perceptions, ask ourselves why we have those perceptions, and proceed as if those perceptions are wrong and really get to know that person we had already judged within seconds based *only* on external perceptions of that person.

Especially during the BLM and Stop Asian Hate movements, it could sometimes be difficult for a multiracial person to determine where we fit into the picture. Instead of being concerned with one's own self, take account of the injustices others have experienced, and be an advocate—not for a particular race, culture, or heritage but for humanity and for seeing others based on their own unique contributions to the world, whatever that may be: friendship, thoughtfulness, kindness, open-mindedness, what that person's values are, and why they have those values.

**

As a senior in high school, my English teacher Mrs. Zitto went around the classroom one day and asked each person what they thought was the best gift they brought to the class during their time in high school. All my classmates seemed to have their own "thing"—a sport, an art, an academic pursuit, or even a relationship or family that was well-known in the community. Being a "new girl" in my sophomore year, I was primarily focused during those three years at Charlotte Catholic on just trying to make friends and getting good grades. Frankly, I did not ever have a "thing" I was known for (that I knew of). Going around the room, each classmate referenced their respective "things"—football, cheerleading, track, theater, chorus, IQ ... When Mrs. Zitto got to me, I was embarrassed because I did not know what to say.

To provide background, during my senior year, Mrs. Zitto and I had spent a great deal of time together, drafting my college essays. There was even one incident where she accidentally forgot to hit "save" on one of my long essay drafts we had worked on for hours. You can imagine how upset we both were after that day; however, we powered through and continued to work together, successfully drafting each of my college admissions essays together. I credit Mrs. Zitto for me getting into the colleges I most wanted to get into.

Anyway, in response to Mrs. Zitto's question about the gift I brought to my class, I was silent—so embarrassed I did not have a specific sport or accolade to talk about—and the rest of the class started laughing. Mrs. Zitto interrupted the laughter and said, "Lexi, I know the gift you have brought this class, and it is a very important one: friendship." I looked at Mrs. Zitto and almost started crying due to a combination of the fact that this did not feel like it was a real "gift" and because she just said something so kind and genuine in front of the whole class. Years after Mrs. Zitto's

English class, I truly believe that gift of friendship has been the most important, memorable, and enduring one of all.

Isn't it ironic that the things in life we compare while we are alive mean little to nothing once we are dead? For example, people are constantly comparing job titles, how attractive their significant other is compared to friends' significant others, cars, houses, how much money is in one's bank account. Once someone dies, their obituary makes no mention of any of these things they spent their entire lives comparing. The main focus of most obituaries is: what values that person held, how they cared for loved ones and others in the community, their generosity, and, overall, the relationships and impact they made throughout time on this Earth. None of that has to do with anything we compete over during our time alive, which is both an irony and tragedy for the human race. This explains why many of the happiest people have almost nothing. Not to get all philosophical on you, but the whole point here is to say we need to care more about what a person stands for to really judge that person instead of creating concrete perceptions based solely on external appearances or any other things we may see or hear about a person.

Don't let anyone make you feel inadequate because you are of mixed race. Now more than ever before, we should see each other as the people we are and what we can do for society and the world. As predicted by *National Geographic*, the "average American" in 2050 will look like a mixed-race individual—people who look like you are only going to increase in the population in the future.[106] You are not alone. Your feelings are valid. Your ambiguity is the beauty of America.

Endnotes

1 Vanessa McGee, "What Does It Mean to Be Multiracial?" Best Colleges.com, published November 8, 2021, https://www.bestcolleges.com/blog/what-is-multiracial/.

2 ——.

3 Alexandra Yoon-Hendricks, "Seattle Public Schools Offers New Filipino American History Class," *Seattle Times*, October 31, 2022, https://www. seattletimes.com/seattle-news/education/seattle-public-schools-offers-new-filipino-american-history-class/.

4 "Elephant in the room," Merriam-Webster.com, accessed September 2, 2020, https://www.merriam-webster.com/dictionary/elephant%20in%20the%20 room.

5 "Identity," *Psychology Today*, accessed September 2, 2020, https://www. psychologytoday.com/us/basics/identity.

6 Saul Mcleod, PhD, "Maslow's Hierarchy of Needs," Simply Psychology, updated April 4, 2022, https://www.simplypsychology.org/maslow.html.

7 Michelle Norris, "Visualizing Race, Identity, and Change," *National Geographic*, published September 17, 2013, https://www.nationalgeographic. com/photography/article/visualizing-change.

8 Jonathan B. Freeman, Kristin Pauker, and Diana T. Sanchez, "A Perceptual Pathway to Bias: Interracial Exposure Reduces Abruptly Shifts in Real-Time Race Perception That Predict Mixed-Race Bias," *Psychological Science* 27, no. 4 (March 2016), https://doi.org/10.1177/095679761562741.

9 Rochelle Younan-Mongomery, "A Point of View: Mixed Race Experience Is Hard to Categorize. Stop Trying" (blog), Inclusion Solution, May 27, 2021,

http://www.theinclusionsolution.me/a-point-of-view-mixed-race-experience-is-hard-to-categorize-stop-trying/.

10 Family Institute at Northwestern University, "Multiracial Identity Development: Illuminating Influential Factor," Newswise, October 12, 2017, https://www.newswise.com/articles/multiracial-identity-development-illuminating-influential-factor.

11 Mahogany L. Swanson, "So, What Are You Anyway?" CYF News, August 2013, https://www.apa.org/pi/families/resources/newsletter/2013/08/biracial-identity.

12 Ariane Resnick, "What Is Racial Ambiguity?" Racism, Very Well Mind, updated June 1, 2021, https://www.verywellmind.com/what-is-racial-ambiguity-5185536.

13 ——.

14 J. D. Remedios and A. L. Chasteen, "Finally, Someone Who 'Gets' Me! Multiracial People Value Others' Accuracy about Their Race," *Cultural Diversity and Ethnic Minority Psychology* 19, no. 4 (2013): 453–60, https://doi.org/10.1037/a0032249.

15 ——.

16 ——, 453.

17 ——.

18 ——, 453–4.

19 ——, 454.

20 ——, 458.

21 Jasmine Norman, "The Racial Identities Multiracial People Adopt May Depend on How Others Treat Them" (blog), Society for Personality and Social Psychology, January 22, 2020, https://www.spsp.org/news-center/blog/norman-multiracial-people-identities.

22 ——.

23 ——.

24 Cynthia Silva Parker and Jen Willsea, "Summary of Stages of Racial Identity Development," Interaction Institute for Social Change, accessed September 2, 2020, https://overcomingracism.org/wp-content/uploads/2021/05/stages-of-racial-identity-development-oct2019.pdf.

25 ——.

26 ——.

27 "College ACB," Wikipedia, accessed October 15, 2022, https://en.wikipedia.org/wiki/College_ACB.

28 Family Institute at Northwestern University, "Multiracial Identity Development."

29 Kim Parker et al., "The Multiracial Identity Gap," chap. 3 in *Multiracial in America* (Washington, DC: Pew Research Center, 2015); and ——, "The Multiracial Experience," chap. 4 in *Multiracial in America* (Washington, DC: Pew Research Center, 2015).

30 ——, "Multiracial Identity Gap."

31 ——.

32 ——.

33 ——, "Multiracial Experience."

34 "Assimilation," Dictionary.com, accessed September 2, 2020, https://www.dictionary.com/browse/assimilation.

35 "Acculturation," Dictionary.com, accessed September 2, 2020, https://www.dictionary.com/browse/acculturation.

36 Mary C. Waters and Marisa Gerstein Pineau, eds., *The Integration of Immigrants into American Society* (Washington, DC: National Academies Press, 2015), https://doi.org/10.17226/21746.

37 Lindsey Kupfer, "Shay Mitchell Tried to Hide Her Filipino Heritage While Growing Up," *Page Six*, January 14, 2015, https://pagesix.com/2015/01/14/shay-mitchell-tried-to-hide-her-filipino-heritage-while-growing-up/.

38 Kayla Greaves, "Shay Mitchell Shared Her Heartbreaking Struggles with the Lack of Asian Representation in Beauty," *Elite Daily*, June 14, 2018, https://www.elitedaily.com/p/shay-mitchells-thoughts-on-representation-in-beauty-are-something-we-all-need-to-hear-9409064.

39 Andrea Mandell, "Meghan Markle Pens a Revealing Essay on Being Biracial in Hollywood," *USA Today*, published December 12, 2016, 5:49 p.m. ET, updated December 13, 2016, 7:48 a.m. ET, https://www.usatoday.com/story/life/people/2016/12/12/meghan-markle-pens-essay-being-biracial-hollywood-prince-harry/95352416/.

40 ——.

41 ——.

42 Katie O'Malley, "Meghan Markle Opens Up about 'Ethnically Ambiguous' Childhood Ahead of Romantic Trip to Botswana," *ELLE*, August 7, 2017, https://www.elle.com/uk/life-and-culture/culture/news/a37569/meghan-markle-race-childhood-botswana-prince-harry/.

43 Jason Pham, "Chrissy Teigen Was Once Embarrassed by Her Ethnic Culture," She Knows, April 5, 2018, https://www.sheknows.com/entertainment/articles/1138993/chrissy-teigen-luna-racial-diversity/.

44 ——.

45 Celeste Katz Marston, "'What Are You?' How Multiracial Americans Respond and How It's Changing," *NBC News*, February 28, 2021, https://www.nbcnews.com/news/asian-america/what-are-you-how-multiracial-americans-respond-how-it-s-n1255166.

46 Stacy L. Smith, Marc Choueiti, and Katherine Pieper, *Inclusion or Invisibility? Comprehensive Annenberg Report on Diversity in Entertainment* (Los Angeles: USC Annenberg School for Communication and Journalism, 2016), https://annenberg.usc.edu/sites/default/files/2017/04/07/MDSCI_CARD_Report_FINAL_Exec_Summary.pdf.

47 ——.

48 Isabel Molina-Guzmán, "#Oscarssowhite: How Stuart Hall Explains Why Nothing Changes in Hollywood and Everything Is Changing," *Critical Studies in Media Communication* 33, no. 5 (2016): 438–54, https://doi.org/1 0.1080/15295036.2016.1227864.

49 ——.

50 ——.

51 Sayaka Osanami Törngren, Nahikari Irastorza, and Dan Rodríguez-García, "Understanding Multiethnic and Multiracial Experiences Globally: Toward a Conceptual Framework of Mixedness," *Journal of Ethnic and Migration Studies* 47, no. 4 (2019): 763–81, https://doi.org/10.1080/136918 3X.2019.1654150.

52 America Ferrera, ed., *American like Me: Reflections on Life Between Cultures* (New York: Gallery Books, 2019).

53 "Racial Justice Helpful Terminology," St. Thomas the Apostle Catholic Church, accessed September 2, 2020, https://www.stapostle.org/racial-justice-helpful-terminology/.

54 ——.

55 ——.

56 Anna Purna Kambhampaty, "'I Will Not Stand Silent.' Ten Asian Americans Reflect on Racism During the Pandemic and the Need for Equality," *TIME*, June 25, 2020, https://time.com/5858649/racism-coronavirus/.

57 Vernon D. Johnson and Kelsie Benslimane, "Practical Representation and the Multiracial Social Movement," *Journal of Educational Controversy* 12, no. 1 (2017), https://cedar.wwu.edu/cgi/viewcontent. cgi?article=1291&context=jec.

58 "White Paper," Merriam-Webster.com, accessed September 2, 2022, https:// www.merriam-webster.com/dictionary/white%20paper.

59 Johnson and Benslimane, "Practical Representation."

60 Kimmy Yam, "Anti-Asian Hate Crimes Increased by Nearly 150 Percent in 2020, Mostly in New York and LA, New Report Says," *NBC News*, March 9, 2021, https://www.nbcnews.com/news/asian-america/anti-asian-hate-crimes-increased-nearly-150-2020-mostly-n-n1260264.

61 Julia Reinstein, "There Have Been at Least 3,795 Hate Incidents Against Asian Americans During the Pandemic, a New Report Shows," BuzzFeed News, March 16, 2021, https://www.buzzfeednews.com/article/juliareinstein/ anti-asian-racist-hate-incidents.

62 Robert Polner, "Pandemic Era Sparks Both Anxiety and Activism for Asian Americans," News Story, nyu.edu, February 26, 2021, https://www.nyu.edu/about/news-publications/news/2021/february/ AsianAmericanDiscriminationStudy.html.

63 Richard Fausset, Nicholas Bogel-Burroughs, and Marie Fazio, "Eight Dead in Atlanta Spa Shootings, with Fears of Anti-Asian Bias," *New York Times*,

published March 17, 2021, updated March 26, 2021, https://www.nytimes.com/live/2021/03/17/us/shooting-atlanta-acworth.

64 Sam Cabral, "Covid 'Hate Crimes' Against Asian Americans on Rise," *BBC News*, May 21, 2021, https://www.bbc.com/news/world-us-canada-56218684.

65 ——.

66 Barbara Sprunt, "Here's What the New Hate Crimes Law Aims to Do as Attacks on Asian Americans Rise," Politics, NPR, updated May 20, 2021, https://www.npr.org/2021/05/20/998599775/biden-to-sign-the-covid-19-hate-crimes-bill-as-anti-asian-american-attacks-rise.

67 Condemning All Forms of Anti-Asian Sentiment as Related to COVID-19, H.R. 151, 17th Cong. (2021) at https://www.congress.gov/bill/117th-congress/house-resolution/151.

68 Sarah E. Gaither, "My Message to Biracial People Questioning Their Role in Black Lives Matter," *Today*, June 30, 2020, https://www.today.com/tmrw/biracial-people-questioning-their-role-black-lives-matter-t185441.

69 ——.

70 Simone Stewart, "Black Lives Matter: Mixed-Race People Share Their Stories," *BBC News*, July 21, 2020, video, 5:02, https://www.bbc.com/news/av/uk-england-53472395.

71 ——.

72 ——.

73 ——.

74 ——.

75 Zara Abrams, "The Mental Health Impact of Anti-Asian Racism," *American Psychological Association* 52, no. 5 (July 2021): 22, https://www.apa.org/monitor/2021/07/impact-anti-asian-racism.

76 ——.

77 Juliana Menasce Horowitz, Anna Brown, and Kiana Cox, "The Role of Race and Ethnicity in Americans' Personal Lives," chap. 3 in *Race in America 2019* (Washington, DC: Pew Research Center, 2019), https://www.pewresearch.org/social-trends/2019/04/09/the-role-of-race-and-ethnicity-in-americans-personal-lives/.

78 Vox First Person, "The Loneliness of Being Mixed Race in America," *Vox*, January 18, 2021, https://www.vox.com/first-person/21734156/kamala-harris-mixed-race-biracial-multiracial.

79 ——.

80 Parker and Willsea, "Summary of Stages."

81 Vox First Person, "The Loneliness."

82 ——.

83 Parker and Willsea, "Summary of Stages."

84 Jennifer Cheang, "Why Imposter Syndrome Goes Deep for Multiracial People" (blog), Mental Health America, August 10, 2020, https://mhanational.org/blog/why-imposter-syndrome-goes-deep-multiracial-people.

85 Mark Twain, *The Innocents Abroad* (London: Harper & Brothers Publishers, 1973).

86 "A Quote by Miriam Beard," Goodreads, accessed July 10, 2022, https://www.goodreads.com/quotes/497207-certainly-travel-is-more-than-the-seeing-of-sights-it.

87 Sara Holtz, "Episode 68: Discovering Your Strengths," November 2018, in *Advice to My Younger Me*, podcast, audio, 10:57, https://tomyyounger.me/.

88 ——, *Advice to My Younger Me* (Austin: Lioncrest Publishing, 2022).

89 Parker, "Multiracial Experience."

90 Alicia del Prado, PhD, "Growing Up Multiracial," *Psychology Today*, November 2, 2019, https://www.psychologytoday.com/us/blog/speaking-the-heart/201911/growing-multiracial.

91 Norris, "Visualizing Race."

92 Dania Santana, "Bill of Rights for People of Mixed Heritage by Maria P. P. Root, PhD," Embracing Diversity, December 10, 2018, https://embracingdiversity.us/bill-of-rights-for-people-of-mixed-heritage-maria-p-p-root-ph-d/.

93 Maria P. P. Root, PhD, *Bill of Rights for People of Mixed Heritage* (Washington, DC: American Psychological Association, 1993), https://www.apa.org/pubs/videos/4310742-rights.pdf.

94 Resnick, "Racial Ambiguity."

95 Johnson and Benslimane, "Practical Representation."

96 Parker, "Multiracial Experience."

97 Cheang, "Imposter Syndrome."

98 Smith, Choueiti, and Pieper, *Inclusion or Invisibility*.

99 Molina-Guzmán, "#Oscarssowhite."

100 McGee, "What Does."

101 Family Institute at Northwestern University, "Multiracial Identity."

102 "Hapa.me: Fifteen Years of the Hapa Project," Past Exhibition, Japanese American National Museum, accessed November 30, 2021, https://www.janm.org/exhibits/hapa-me.

103 Dan Schindel, "How Our Conversations Around Mixed-Race Identity Have Evolved in the 21st Century," Art, Hyperallergic, July 9, 2018, https://hyperallergic.com/450093/hapa-me-project-kip-fulbeck-japanese-american-national-museum/.

104 Remedios and Chasteen, "'Gets' Me."

105 ——.

106 Norris, "Visualizing."

Bibliography

"A Quote by Miriam Beard." Goodreads. Accessed July 10, 2022.
https://www.goodreads.com/quotes/497207-certainly-travel-is-more-than-the-seeing-of-sights-it.

"Acculturation." Dictionary.com. Accessed September 2, 2020. https://www.dictionary.com/browse/acculturation.

"Assimilation." Dictionary.com. Accessed September 2, 2020. https://www.dictionary.com/browse/assimilation.

"College ACB." Wikipedia. Accessed October 15, 2022. https://en.wikipedia.org/wiki/College_ACB.

"Elephant in the room." Merriam-Webster.com. Accessed September 2, 2020.
https://www.merriam-webster.com/dictionary/elephant%20in%20the%20room.

"Hapa.me: Fifteen Years of the Hapa Project." Past Exhibition. Japanese American National Museum. Accessed November 30, 2021. https://www.janm.org/exhibits/hapa-me.

"Identity." *Psychology Today*. Accessed September 2, 2020. https://www.psychologytoday.com/us/basics/identity.

"Racial Justice Helpful Terminology." St. Thomas the Apostle Catholic Church. Accessed September 2, 2020. https://www.stapostle.org/racial-justice-helpful-terminology/.

"White Paper." Merriam-Webster.com. Accessed September 2, 2022. https://www.merriam-webster.com/dictionary/white%20paper.

Abrams, Zara. "The Mental Health Impact of Anti-Asian Racism." *American Psychological Association* 52, no. 5 (July 2021): 22. https://www.apa.org/monitor/2021/07/impact-anti-asian-racism.

Cabral, Sam. "Covid 'Hate Crimes' Against Asian Americans on Rise." *BBC News*. May 21, 2021. https://www.bbc.com/news/world-us-canada-56218684.

Cheang, Jennifer. "Why Imposter Syndrome Goes Deep for Multiracial People" (blog). Mental Health America. August 10, 2020. https://mhanational.org/blog/why-imposter-syndrome-goes-deep-multiracial-people.

Condemning All Forms of Anti-Asian Sentiment as Related to COVID-19. H.R. 151. 17th Cong. (2021) at https://www.congress.gov/bill/117th-congress/house-resolution/151.

Del Prado, Alicia, PhD. "Growing Up Multiracial." *Psychology Today*. November 2, 2019. https://www.psychologytoday.com/us/blog/speaking-the-heart/201911/growing-multiracial.

Family Institute at Northwestern University. "Multiracial Identity Development: Illuminating Influential Factor." *Newswise*. October 12, 2017. https://www.newswise.com/articles/multiracial-identity-development-illuminating-influential-factor.

Fausset, Richard, Nicholas Bogel-Burroughs, and Marie Fazio. "Eight Dead in Atlanta Spa Shootings, with Fears of Anti-Asian Bias." *New York Times*. Published March 17, 2021. Updated March 26, 2021. https://www.nytimes.com/live/2021/03/17/us/shooting-atlanta-acworth.

Ferrera, America, ed. *American like Me: Reflections on Life Between Cultures*. New York: Gallery Books, 2019.

Freeman, Jonathan B., Kristin Pauker, and Diana T. Sanchez. "A Perceptual Pathway to Bias: Interracial Exposure Reduces Abruptly Shifts in Real-Time Race Perception That Predict Mixed-Race Bias." *Psychological Science* 27, no. 4 (March 2016). https://doi.org/10.1177/095679761562741.

Gaither, Sarah E. "My Message to Biracial People Questioning Their Role in Black Lives Matter." *Today*. June 30, 2020. https://www.today.com/tmrw/biracial-people-questioning-their-role-black-lives-matter-t185441.

Greaves, Kayla. "Shay Mitchell Shared Her Heartbreaking Struggles with the Lack of Asian Representation in Beauty." *Elite Daily*. June 14, 2018. https://www.elitedaily.com/p/shay-mitchells-thoughts-on-representation-in-beauty-are-something-we-all-need-to-hear-9409064.

Holtz, Sara. "Episode 68: Discovering Your Strengths." November 2018. In *Advice to My Younger Me*. Podcast. Audio. 10:57. https://tomyyounger.me/.

——. *Advice to My Younger Me*. Austin: Lioncrest Publishing, 2022.

Horowitz, Juliana Menasce, Anna Brown, and Kiana Cox. "The Role of Race and Ethnicity in Americans' Personal Lives." Chap. 3 in *Race in America 2019*. Washington, DC: Pew Research Center, 2019. https://www.pewresearch.org/social-trends/2019/04/09/the-role-of-race-and-ethnicity-in-americans-personal-lives/.

Johnson, Vernon D., and Kelsie Benslimane. "Practical Representation and the Multiracial Social Movement." *Journal of Educational Controversy* 12, no. 1 (2017). https://cedar.wwu.edu/cgi/viewcontent.cgi?article=1291&context=jec.

Kambhampaty, Anna Purna. "'I Will Not Stand Silent.' Ten Asian Americans Reflect on Racism During the Pandemic and the Need for Equality." *TIME*. June 25, 2020. https://time.com/5858649/racism-coronavirus/.

Kupfer, Lindsey. "Shay Mitchell Tried to Hide Her Filipino Heritage While Growing Up." *Page Six*. January 14, 2015. https://pagesix.com/2015/01/14/shay-mitchell-tried-to-hide-her-filipino-heritage-while-growing-up/.

Mandell, Andrea. "Meghan Markle Pens a Revealing Essay on Being Biracial in Hollywood." *USA Today*. Published December 12, 2016, 5:49 p.m. ET. Updated December 13, 2016, 7:48 a.m. ET. https://www.usatoday.com/story/life/people/2016/12/12/meghan-markle-pens-essay-being-biracial-hollywood-prince-harry/95352416/.

Marston, Celeste Katz. "'What Are You?' How Multiracial Americans Respond and How It's Changing." *NBC News*. February 28, 2021. https://www.nbcnews.com/news/asian-america/what-are-you-how-multiracial-americans-respond-how-it-s-n1255166.

McGee, Vanessa. "What Does It Mean to Be Multiracial?" Best Colleges.com. Published November 8, 2021. https://www.bestcolleges.com/blog/what-is-multiracial/.

Mcleod, Saul, PhD. "Maslow's Hierarchy of Needs." *Simply Psychology*. Updated April 4, 2022. https://www.simplypsychology.org/maslow.html.

Molina-Guzmán, Isabel. "#Oscarssowhite: How Stuart Hall Explains Why Nothing Changes in Hollywood and Everything Is Changing." *Critical Studies in Media Communication* 33, no. 5 (2016): 438–54. https://doi.org/10.1080/15295036.2016.1227864.

Norman, Jasmine. "The Racial Identities Multiracial People Adopt May Depend on How Others Treat Them" (blog). Society for Personality and Social Psychology. Posted January 22, 2020. https://www.spsp.org/news-center/blog/norman-multiracial-people-identities.

Norris, Michelle. "Visualizing Race, Identity, and Change." *National Geographic*. Published September 17, 2013. https://www.nationalgeographic.com/photography/article/visualizing-change.

O'Malley, Katie. "Meghan Markle Opens Up about 'Ethnically Ambiguous' Childhood Ahead of Romantic Trip to Botswana." *ELLE*. August 7, 2017. https://www.elle.com/uk/life-and-culture/culture/news/a37569/meghan-markle-race-childhood-botswana-prince-harry/.

Parker, Cynthia Silva, and Jen Willsea. "Summary of Stages of Racial Identity Development." Interaction Institute for Social Change. Accessed September 2, 2020. https://overcomingracism.org/wp-content/uploads/2021/05/stages-of-racial-identity-development-oct2019.pdf.

Parker, Kim, Juliana Menasce Horowitz, Rich Morin, and Mark Hugo Lopez. "The Multiracial Identity Gap." Chap. 3 in *Multiracial in America*. Washington, DC: Pew Research Center, 2015.

——. "The Multiracial Experience." Chap. 4 in *Multiracial in America*. Washington, DC: Pew Research Center, 2015.

Pham, Jason. "Chrissy Teigen Was Once Embarrassed by Her Ethnic Culture." She Knows. April 5, 2018. https://www.sheknows.com/entertainment/articles/1138993/chrissy-teigen-luna-racial-diversity/.

Polner, Robert. "Pandemic Era Sparks Both Anxiety and Activism for Asian Americans." News Story. Nyu.edu. February 26, 2021. https://www.nyu.edu/about/news-publications/news/2021/february/AsianAmericanDiscriminationStudy.html.

Reinstein, Julia. "There Have Been at Least 3,795 Hate Incidents Against Asian Americans During the Pandemic, a New Report Shows." BuzzFeed News. March 16, 2021. https://www.buzzfeednews.com/article/juliareinstein/anti-asian-racist-hate-incidents.

Remedios, J. D., and A. L. Chasteen. "Finally, Someone Who 'Gets' Me! Multiracial People Value Others' Accuracy about Their Race." *Cultural Diversity and Ethnic Minority Psychology* 19, no. 4 (2013): 453–60. https://doi.org/10.1037/a0032249.

Resnick, Ariane. "What Is Racial Ambiguity?" Racism. Very Well Mind. Updated June 1, 2021. https://www.verywellmind.com/what-is-racial-ambiguity-5185536.

Root, Maria P. P., PhD. *Bill of Rights for People of Mixed Heritage*. Washington, DC: American Psychological Association, 1993. https://www.apa.org/pubs/videos/4310742-rights.pdf.

Santana, Dania. "Bill of Rights for People of Mixed Heritage by Maria P. P. Root, PhD." Embracing Diversity. December 10, 2018. https://embracingdiversity.us/bill-of-rights-for-people-of-mixed-heritage-maria-p-p-root-ph-d/.

Schindel, Dan. "How Our Conversations Around Mixed-Race Identity Have Evolved in the 21st Century." Art. Hyperallergic. July 9, 2018. https://hyperallergic.com/450093/hapa-me-project-kip-fulbeck-japanese-american-national-museum/.

Smith, Stacy L., Marc Choueiti, and Katherine Pieper. *Inclusion or Invisibility? Comprehensive Annenberg Report on Diversity in Entertainment*. Los Angeles: USC Annenberg School for Communication and Journalism, 2016. https://annenberg.usc.edu/sites/default/files/2017/04/07/MDSCI_CARD_Report_FINAL_Exec_Summary.pdf.

Sprunt, Barbara. "Here's What the New Hate Crimes Law Aims to Do as Attacks on Asian Americans Rise." Politics. NPR. Updated May 20, 2021. https://www.npr.org/2021/05/20/998599775/biden-to-sign-the-covid-19-hate-crimes-bill-as-anti-asian-american-attacks-rise.

Stewart, Simone. "Black Lives Matter: Mixed-Race People Share Their Stories." *BBC News*. July 21, 2020. Video. 5:02. https://www.bbc.com/news/av/uk-england-53472395.

Swanson, Mahogany L. "So, What Are You Anyway?" *CYF News*. Posted August 2013. https://www.apa.org/pi/families/resources/newsletter/2013/08/biracial-identity.

Törngren, Sayaka Osanami, Nahikari Irastorza, and Dan Rodríguez-García. "Understanding Multiethnic and Multiracial Experiences Globally: Toward a Conceptual Framework of Mixedness." *Journal of Ethnic and Migration Studies* 47, no. 4 (2019): 763–81. https://doi.org/10.1080/1369183X.2019.1654150.

Twain, Mark. *The Innocents Abroad*. London: Harper & Brothers Publishers, 1973.

Vox First Person. "The Loneliness of Being Mixed Race in America." *Vox*. January 18, 2021. https://www.vox.com/first-person/21734156/kamala-harris-mixed-race-biracial-multiracial.

Waters, Mary C., and Marisa Gerstein Pineau, eds. *The Integration of Immigrants into American Society*. Washington, DC: National Academies Press, 2015. https://doi.org/10.17226/21746.

Yam, Kimmy. "Anti-Asian Hate Crimes Increased by Nearly 150 Percent in 2020, Mostly in New York and LA, New Report Says." *NBC News*. March 9, 2021. https://www.nbcnews.com/news/asian-america/anti-asian-hate-crimes-increased-nearly-150-2020-mostly-n-n1260264.

Yoon-Hendricks, Alexandra. "Seattle Public Schools Offers New Filipino American History Class." *Seattle Times*. October 31, 2022. https://www.seattletimes.com/seattle-news/education/seattle-public-schools-offers-new-filipino-american-history-class/.

Younan-Mongomery, Rochelle. "A Point of View: Mixed Race Experience Is Hard to Categorize. Stop Trying" (blog). Inclusion Solution. May 27, 2021. http://www.theinclusionsolution.me/a-point-of-view-mixed-race-experience-is-hard-to-categorize-stop-trying/.